SHAKESPEARE

A BEGINNER'S GUIDE

RONI JAY

Hodder & Stoughton

A MEMBER OF THE HODDER HEADLINE GROUP

Orders: please contact Bookpoint Ltd, 78 Milton Park, Abingdon, Oxon OX14 4TD. Telephone: (44) 01235 827720, Fax: (44) 01235 400454. Lines are open from 9.00–6.00, Monday to Saturday, with a 24-hour message answering service. Email address: orders@bookpoint.co.uk

British Library Cataloguing in Publication Data
A catalogue record for this title is available from The British Library

ISBN 0 340 78010 X

First published 2000
Impression number   10 9 8 7 6 5 4 3 2 1
Year   2005 2004 2003 2002 2001 2000

Cartoons by Richard Chapman
Typeset by Transet Limited, Coventry, England.
Printed in Great Britain for Hodder & Stoughton Educational, a division of Hodder Headline plc, 338 Euston Road, London NW1 3BH by Cox & Wyman, Reading, Berks

CONTENTS

Contents

Who was Shakespeare?

In many ways, William Shakespeare's life is something of a mystery. Considering that he is the world's best known playwright, we know surprisingly little about his private life. What's more, many people find it so unlikely that someone of such modest origins should have been so skilled a writer, that they claim William Shakespeare didn't write the plays at all. They argue that someone else wrote the plays and poems, and used Shakespeare's name and identity as a cover.

We'll look at the case for this in a moment, and at the main contenders who are variously claimed to have written the plays. But first of all, let's look at the official (and, frankly, by far the most likely) version. Nobody doubts Shakespeare's existence, or his life in the theatre; they only question who was really writing the plays.

FROM STRATFORD TO LONDON

William Shakespeare was born in Stratford-upon-Avon in Warwickshire, England, in 1564. His father, John, came from a farming family but trained as a glove-maker. He did rather well for himself – branching out into wool dealing and money-lending as well – and married Mary Arden, whose family were minor gentry and well respected in the area. Business was good enough for him to buy two houses in the centre of Stratford, where William was born – their first surviving child (they had lost two).

KEY FACTS

There was no birth certificate when Shakespeare was born to give an exact date of birth, but there was an entry in the church register of the baptism. Shakespeare was baptized on 26 April 1564. Since babies were generally baptized at around three days old, he was most likely born on 23 April.

Much the same applies to his death. He was buried on 25 April 1616, and burials usually took place about two days after death. So he probably died on 23 April, which was the most likely date of his birthday. For the sake of argument, it is traditionally assumed that he was born and died on the same day, and his life is always celebrated on 23 April.

John and Mary Shakespeare went on to have five more children (one of whom died young), so William grew up as the eldest of a large family. He almost certainly went to the local grammar school (which is still there), although we have no way of knowing for certain. However, he would have learnt a little Latin and Greek, and studied classical writers, which would explain where he got many of the plots and ideas for his plays from (as we'll see in Chapter 5).

SHOTGUN WEDDING

Shakespeare would have left school at 14, and we've no idea what happened to him for the next four years. When he was 18, however, he married Anne Hathaway, who was the daughter of a local farmer and eight years older than him. He married her in November 1582; their daughter Susanna was baptized six months later. In 1584 Anne gave birth to twins, Judith and Hamnet. For the next seven years Shakespeare disappears from the history books, to reappear in London in 1592.

We have no idea what happened during these 'missing' years, but not surprisingly there are plenty of stories and theories. One suggestion, which seems quite plausible, is that he became a schoolmaster. Another story is that he was caught poaching in nearby Charlecote Park, and ran away to London to avoid prosecution. Certainly he would have had the opportunity to acquire a taste for the theatre. As well as plenty of local amateur shows, Shakespeare would have seen touring shows from London which visited regularly. He may even have joined one of the companies.

A CAREER IN THE THEATRE

It seems likely that Shakespeare arrived in London in the late 1580s, but all we really know for certain is that by the early 1590s he was in London and becoming an established writer. A fellow dramatist, named Robert Greene, is recorded as having described Shakespeare as 'an upstart crow' in 1592: the 28-year-old from Stratford was clearly becoming prominent.

The first works Shakespeare had published were two long poems: *Venus and Adonis* in 1593 followed by *The Rape of Lucrece* in 1594. Both of these were dedicated to his **patron**, the Earl of Southampton, who was one of Queen Elizabeth I's favourite courtiers.

In 1594, Shakespeare joined a new acting company that was being formed by Richard Burbage. He stayed with this company for the next twenty years, as an actor and as its regular playwright. Burbage played the lead roles, but Shakespeare played many parts, both comic and tragic, and was by all accounts a good actor.

KEYWORD

Patron: a champion or benefactor. Henry Wriothsely, Earl of Southampton, would not only have encouraged and publicly praised and recommended Shakespeare, but also given him valuable introductions and financial help. He once gave Shakespeare a thousand pounds (an enormous sum at the time) because he had heard that Shakespeare wanted to buy something at that price.

Burbage's company often played in front of Queen Elizabeth I and, when she died in 1603, James I granted royal patronage to the company, who became known as the King's Men. In 1609 the King's Men acquired the luxury of an indoor theatre, the Blackfriars, as well as performing at the Globe, both situated near to the city of London.

SHAKESPEARE'S HOME LIFE

Shakespeare's wife and children spent their lives in Stratford-upon-Avon, and Shakespeare presumably returned there fairly regularly. He was becoming wealthy, largely due to his shares in the Globe Theatre and in 1597 he bought one of Stratford's biggest houses, New Place. His father, John, was mayor of the town and was granted a coat-of-arms, which William inherited on his father's death in 1601. This made him officially a 'gentleman', despite being a mere 'theatrical'.

Shakespeare went on to buy other land and property in Stratford, and seems to have maintained his links with the town. He is said to have been heartbroken at the death of his son, Hamnet, at the age of eleven. After about 1611, Shakespeare largely separated himself from the

London theatre world, and spent most of his time in Stratford. He made his will shortly before his death, dividing his property between his family and friends, including three of his colleagues in the King's Men (and famously leaving his wife his 'second-best bed').

In 1616, Shakespeare died and was buried in Holy Trinity Church in Stratford. A bust, which is still there, was put up on the wall nearby shortly afterwards. His grave is covered with a stone which bears the inscription:

Good friend, for Jesus' sake forbear
To dig the dust enclosed here
Blessed be the man that spares these stones
And cursed be he that moves my bones.

THE SHAKESPEARE AUTHORSHIP DEBATE

Since the Eighteenth Century, many people have argued that the plays we traditionally attribute to Shakespeare were actually written by someone else entirely. Most of these people accept that Shakespeare existed, and worked with Burbage's acting company, but say that he was merely claiming as his own plays those that someone else was passing to him. Some even say that the name Shakespeare was simply a pseudonym, and the William Shakespeare of Stratford-upon-Avon was unconnected with the plays in any way.

The adherents of this view have included such famous names as Sigmund Freud, Henry James, Mark Twain and Benjamin Disraeli. Underlying the various claims, whichever alternative author they support, is the argument that William Shakespeare himself could not have written the plays. The key reasons set out for this are as follows:

* Unlike most other leading writers and dramatists of the time, he did not have a university education (which is one of the reasons he was called an 'upstart crow'). So how would he have acquired the knowledge of the classics, of law and of languages which the plays contain?

* Not one of the well-known poets or dramatists of England who were alive at his death wrote any tribute to him at the time.

* His will, despite its detail, does not itemize any books or manuscripts as belonging to his estate.

These are just a few of the many arguments put forward to support the case that another author wrote Shakespeare's works. Some people have also claimed to have discovered clues and ciphers in the plays which point to another author. But who? Some have argued that the plays were written by Sir Walter Raleigh, by Ben Jonson, or even by Queen Elizabeth I. One theory suggests that the history plays were written by a secret committee of 'university wits'. The aim was supposedly to reinforce Queen Elizabeth's claim to the throne by promoting pro-Tudor propaganda, and also to generate enthusiasm among the (tax-paying) public for the impending war against Spain.

However, three main candidates stand out as being the most popular at the moment.

Christopher Marlowe (1564–93)

Marlowe has been a popular candidate for centuries, and certainly a romantic one. He was arguably the greatest playwright before Shakespeare, and wrote half a dozen plays, the most famous being *Dr Faustus* (1604). He was born in the same year as Shakespeare but died in 1593, at about the same time that Shakespeare's first plays were being produced. He was stabbed to death in a tavern brawl. The argument for his authorship of the plays is that he was actually a government spy (which is possible) and that he didn't really die in the brawl but it was convenient for him to let everyone think he had. So he 'disappeared', but continued to write under Shakespeare's name.

Sir Francis Bacon (1561–1626)

Bacon was a philosopher and writer, and used to be the favourite candidate of the anti-Stratfordians (those who argue Shakespeare wasn't really Shakespeare). He certainly had the education to satisfy those who say

that only a man of great learning could have written the plays. However, his style was very different from that of Shakespeare's plays. It is also unclear why he would not have used his own identity to publish the plays.

Edward de Vere, 17th Earl of Oxford (1550–1604)

The current favourite, first put forward in the 1930s as a possible author of the plays. Certainly he was well-travelled and educated enough to have written them, and many people argue that much of the material in the plays parallels his own life. For example, his own guardian, William Cecil, is strikingly similar in some ways to the character of Polonius in *Hamlet.* He had a great interest in the arts, and was patron of his own acting company and of many writers. The argument is that he used a pseudonym to escape the wrath of the court for allegedly ridiculing it in the plays. Plenty of circumstantial evidence has been produced to support his claim; for example, in 1578 (about 14 years before Shakespeare first appeared on the public scene), one of the writers he patronised, Gabriel Harvey, wrote '…thy countenance shakes a spear'. This line has been quoted as evidence that Shakespeare was de Vere's secret pen name.

The main body of opinion, however, and especially that of the leading Shakespeare scholars, is that there is no reason whatever to disbelieve Shakespeare's authorship of his own plays. Many of the other theories are appealing, even romantic, but there is no evidence for them. Computer matches between the writing style of the plays and the styles of Marlowe, Bacon and de Vere, all show that they simply don't match up at all.

The arguments used to cast doubt on Shakespeare's authorship are generally flawed. There is an argument that he probably didn't attend the grammar school at all, since there is no record of his having done so. However, there are no records at all of anyone attending the school – school records simply weren't kept – but we know the school existed at the time.

Another argument points out that Shakespeare's will makes no record of his having owned any books at all – surprising for a writer. However, there was a detailed inventory of the contents of the house attached to the will, which has since been lost. We have no idea what was in this, but it would have been the most likely place to list his books.

The fact is that we simply don't have enough contemporary documentary evidence either way, simply because Shakespeare lived four hundred years ago and little hard evidence of any kind exists from this time. Francis Bacon didn't mention his library of books in his will either, although we know he had one. There is no good reason at all why Shakespeare the playwright shouldn't have been simply William Shakespeare of Stratford-upon-Avon.

The authorship debate is bound to continue, but in the end, the biggest reason for supporting one of the other candidates is because conspiracy theories are fun, and Shakespeare as Shakespeare is just a bit bland by comparison!

✳ ✳ ✳ ✳*SUMMARY* ✳ ✳ ✳ ✳

- Shakespeare was born in Stratford-upon-Avon in Warwickshire, England, in 1564.

- His father was a successful glover, and Shakespeare probably attended the local grammar school.

- He married at 18 and had three children: Susanna, Judith and Hamnet.

- No one knows what he was doing between 1585 and 1592, but by the end of this period he was working in London as an actor and writer.

- He was a successful playwright in his own lifetime, working for Richard Burbage's company, and performing in front of Queen Elizabeth I and, later, King James I.

- His wife and children remained in Stratford, where he bought one of the biggest houses in town, along with other property.

- He died in Stratford in 1616 and is buried in the church there.

- Some people argue that the plays were actually written by someone else. The chief contenders are Christopher Marlowe, Sir Francis Bacon and Edward de Vere, Earl of Oxford.

The Time of Shakespeare

2

Shakespeare lived during a time of great change, of which he himself was a part. Queen Elizabeth I came to the throne in 1558, six years before Shakespeare's birth, and ruled for the next 45 years, bringing stability to the country at a vital time. During her reign, England became the leading naval and commercial power in the Western world. Culturally, too, England had been caught up in the **Renaissance** movement which had begun in fourteenth century Italy and spread across Europe.

THE POLITICAL SCENE

The politics of the time influenced Shakespeare's writings, especially his historical plays. Elizabeth I had a hard job stabilizing the country. Her father, Henry VIII, had split from the Roman Catholic church and formed the English Church led by the monarch rather than the Pope. Henry resented the Pope's interference in his country's politics (the Church was extremely powerful throughout Europe), and used the Pope's refusal to grant him a divorce from Catherine of Aragon as an excuse to break away.

This meant that the country ceased to be officially Catholic, and Henry dissolved the monasteries and declared that everyone had to follow his newly established Church of England. On his death, his young son Edward VI ruled for a short time, and was also a Protestant. However, he died aged only 16, and his sister Mary became Queen.

Queen Mary I was the daughter of the divorced queen Catherine of Aragon, and married to Philip of Spain, and consequently still supported the Catholic faith. She reasserted the Catholic faith, and her treatment of heretics – those who refused to support Catholicism – was so severe she became known as 'Bloody Mary'. The usual punishment for heresy was execution, generally by burning at the stake.

KEY FACT

Henry VIII was the son of Henry VII, who ended the Wars of the Roses when he wrested the English throne from Richard III in 1485. He actually had a relatively weak claim to the throne, but managed to maintain a firm hold on it nonetheless. He was Elizabeth's grandfather, and came to the throne less than 80 years before Shakespeare was born. So Shakespeare's plays – if he was to be popular with the establishment – needed to support Henry VII and his heirs, and their right to reign. This is why the play *Richard III* paints such a black picture of King Richard.

Mary reigned for only five years before she died, leaving no children. The natural heir to the throne was her sister Elizabeth, Henry's daughter by his second wife, Anne Boleyn. Anne was the woman Henry had wanted to marry when he sought the divorce from Mary's mother, Catherine of Aragon, so she was naturally in favour of the divorce and a Protestant (I hope you're still following this!). Her daughter, Elizabeth, had been brought up in the same faith.

When Elizabeth I succeeded to the throne, she encouraged everyone to revert to Protestantism once again. This 'yo-yoing' between faiths had been bad for the country, stirring up fear, suspicion and resentment, and at least Elizabeth had the sense to adopt a more tolerant view than her sister. However, her position was not really secure until she had proved she was a strong and popular leader. Shakespeare's last play, *Henry VIII*, written in 1613, is about the divorce from both the Catholic Church and Catherine of Aragon. It supports Henry's (and thereby Elizabeth's), claim to the throne, indicating that such propaganda was still considered worthwhile ten years after Elizabeth's death.

Despite Elizabeth's tolerance, political stability was still under threat for most of her reign, not least because she refused to marry and produce an heir. War with either Spain or Ireland threatened with varying degrees of seriousness throughout her reign, and many men served in the army at one time or another. Not surprisingly, soldiers feature in many of Shakespeare's plays, not only in the history plays but in comedies and tragedies too. There is a theory that he was in the army during the 'missing' years.

RELIGIOUS CHANGES

In the early Sixteenth Century, Martin Luther (1483–1546) began to criticize the Catholic Church. He argued that it had strayed from the true teachings of the Bible, and was corrupt and excessively wealthy. He and John Calvin were leaders of two of the key Protestant movements of the time, which formed a break from the established Church and became popular in Germany and northern Europe. This organization of the Church into a new order became known as the Reformation, and it had taken hold firmly by the middle of the Sixteenth Century. It was popular with kings because they kept the Church revenue in their own treasury.

The Reformation was really a by-product of the Renaissance. It was inevitable that as people began to be less overawed by the Church, and to focus on the way they lived this life rather than the next, they would begin to question the Church in a way they hadn't dared to before.

In England, the Reformation took a slightly different course from elsewhere. Henry VIII had jumped on the Protestant bandwagon as a way out of his marriage to Catherine of Aragon, and claimed to be head of the English Church. He didn't really make many other changes, but his son Edward VI was a staunch Protestant and furthered the cause. After Mary's persecution of the Protestants, Elizabeth I tried to keep everyone happy by incorporating both Protestantism and Catholicism into the Church of England, although with the emphasis on Protestantism. She made allowances for Catholicism by retaining the structure of the old Church under the control of bishops in the Catholic style.

KEY FACT

One of the most notable conflicts of Elizabeth's reign was between herself and the Catholic Mary Queen of Scots. The English Catholics, along with the great European Catholic powers of France and Spain, wanted to put Mary on the throne in Elizabeth's place and return the country to the Roman Catholic faith. (Philip II of Spain had been married to Elizabeth's elder sister, Queen Mary – another reason for his animosity to Elizabeth.) Eventually Elizabeth had Mary executed, giving Spain the excuse it needed for war; this is what the Spanish Armada of 1588 was all about. Mary died leaving a son, James, whom Elizabeth made her heir. He ruled England and Scotland as James I during the last quarter of Shakespeare's life.

CULTURAL REBIRTH

The new ideas and inventions of the Renaissance were changing the cultural scene past recognition from the austere religious climate of the Middle Ages. Printing meant that new ideas could be promulgated to anyone who could read; the compass meant that new voyages could be launched to discover new lands; and gunpowder meant that wars could be fought on a grander and more terrible scale.

Now that the focus was on humanity rather than God, painters began to depict people differently. Not only were non-religious paintings now permissible, but even religious paintings could show the human form as beautiful. Sculpture and architecture blossomed too. People became inquisitive, and began to search for knowledge, and modern science began to take root. Great Renaissance minds include Leonardo da Vinci, Michaelangelo, Botticelli, Columbus, Copernicus and Galileo. One of the great late Renaissance philosophers was Francis Bacon (one of the contenders for authorship of Shakespeare's plays – see Chapter 2).

Shakespeare lived during the end of the Renaissance period, and was therefore born into a time when there was great emphasis on learning and intellect, and when new ways were a virtue, not a heresy. Certainly his style of playwriting was a break from tradition.

Before the middle of the sixteenth century, almost the only plays performed were **miracle plays** and **mystery plays**. In these plays, all the characters were either good or evil, and the plots and characters were two-dimensional. Even the first great English playwright, Christopher Marlowe (born in the same year as Shakespeare), tended to portray his characters in black and white. As in earlier theatrical traditions, his characters also spoke in strict rhyming couplets.

Shakespeare, for the first time, broke the rules. It can be hard to appreciate how revolutionary his approach was from today's viewpoint, but at the time it was an entirely new kind of drama. Shakespeare's characters, especially the central ones, are incredibly complex, capable of both good and evil, and of human emotions such as guilt and remorse. The enduring appeal of *Hamlet*, *Othello* and many others, is that we can identify with the central character because they go through similar emotions that we might experience ourselves. Even monarchs are portrayed as being merely human.

> **KEYWORDS**
>
> **Miracle plays/mystery plays:** These were religious dramas, popular in the middle ages, generally performed in the open air by bands of 'mummers' (actors) on a raised platform or simply a cart. A miracle play depicted scenes from the Bible, or the lives of saints and martyrs, while a mystery play presented episodes from the life of Christ.

Although Shakespeare wrote his early plays in rhyming couplets, he quickly started to experiment with other forms, using prose and often abandoning rhyme in his verse except for special effect, such as in the closing lines of a scene. He began to change the way a line scanned, or to put an extra beat in the rhythm, or to leave half a line hanging. His style may seem antiquated and stilted today, but in his own time it would have had the opposite image.

Shakespeare reflected the age in which he lived. He also fuelled it. Theatres in his time were the best places for ordinary people to go to witness an honest commentary on life – and it was ordinary people, not just the social elite, who attended theatres. The authorities were obviously sensitive to this, because theatres were regularly shut down when governments decided they were too subversive. In 1603, when Elizabeth I was dying, the playhouses were closed down as a matter of course to protect against disorder breaking out.

SOCIAL LIFE

To understand the plays of Shakespeare, you also need to understand some of the social conventions of the day. These are evident all through the plays, and would have been second nature to Shakespeare's contemporary audiences, even though they can be hard to grasp now.

Hierarchy was deeply important, and high social position was treated with great respect and deference. At the top of the tree was the monarch, of course. After the monarch came the nobility, who were treated with great ceremony. Shakespeare and his fellow actors would have encountered noblemen, who often became their patrons. Knights were the next in line; Elizabeth created very few of these but her successor, King James, created 900 in his first year alone (this was considered a bit of a joke). The next level in the hierarchy was the gentleman. Officially, this was a man who had been granted (or had inherited) a coat of arms – as happened to Shakespeare – but unofficially a gentleman was anyone of sufficient income. Below the gentlefolk were the common people, who knew their place. They were generally very poor and had a low standard of living.

Men were the head of the household at every point on the social scale. They decided when and whom their daughters should marry, and they demanded respect from their wives and children. Their sons called them 'Sir', and were expected to stand in their presence. There was generally less room for affection and companionship between the generations than there is now; in *Romeo and Juliet*, Capulet's attitude to his daughter Juliet is a good example of this. He indulgently asks her opinion on whether she should marry Paris, but the final decision rests with him.

Women had few rights. When they married, everything they owned passed to their husband (except in exceptional cases when lawyers were involved). This meant that wealthy women, and wealthy widows, were greatly in demand as wives. Hamlet is revolted that his mother should have remarried before the feast from his father's funeral had gone cold, but it was not uncommon for widows to marry so swiftly. The etiquette was clear – it was improper to accept a proposal of marriage while her late husband's body was still in the house.

Shakespeare's plays are far more rewarding to watch with an understanding of the time in which he was writing. Customs that seem outdated, or events which seem unimportant to us, are fresh and relevant if you view the plays through Sixteenth- and early Seventeenth-Century eyes.

✻✻✻SUMMARY✻✻✻

- Shakespeare lived just after a time of huge political upheaval, when stability was still in the process of being re-established.

- The conflict between the Roman Catholic and the Protestant churches was still not resolved, and the Catholic powers were plotting and campaigning to put a Catholic back on the English throne.

- Many of Shakespeare's plays relate to earlier disputes over the succession, and support Elizabeth I and James I's right to the throne.

- Shakespeare lived through the end of the Renaissance, a time when art, philosophy and learning blossomed.

- His plays broke new ground in style and in the way he drew his characters as real people.

- The plays reflect the social hierarchies, conventions and customs of the time he lived in.

3 Shakespeare's Theatre

Shakespeare's plays are read more often than they are seen these days, but it wasn't always like that. When he first wrote them, the only people who read them were the actors. Shakespeare wrote his plays to be performed, and to appreciate the plays fully you need to understand the medium for which he intended them. For instance:

* The famous crowd scene in *Julius Caesar*, in which Brutus persuades the people of Rome to his point of view, and Mark Antony then talks them back round to his way of thinking: not only are the actors playing the part of the Roman people, but the entire audience is also being persuaded this way and that. Shakespeare draws the audience in by treating them as an extension of the Roman crowd.

* In several of the plays, the actors speak directly to the audience, especially in prologues and epilogues. Sometimes these speeches are given by a chorus, who is really a narrator, but sometimes the characters themselves step out of the action to address the audience in a **soliloquy**. If you read the epilogue to *As You Like It*, spoken by Rosalind, you'll find a good example of this.

* Shakespeare's soliloquies are written very much with the audience in mind. The characters are talking not only to themselves, but also to us.

> **KEYWORD**
>
> Soliloquy: a speech by a character who is thinking aloud, usually alone on stage. The audience is allowed to hear the character's thoughts, making the soliloquy a valuable theatrical trick. It gives the audience an insight into feelings which the character would not reveal in dialogue with any of the other characters. Shakespeare's most famous soliloquy is probably Hamlet's speech which begins, 'To be or not to be: that is the question.'

THE THEATRE BUILDINGS

Elizabethan theatres were mostly open to the sky, with a stage jutting out into the central arena where the bulk of the audience stood (and Elizabethan weather was worse than it is today!). The area behind the stage was closed off for the actors' use, while galleried seating – with a roof – ran round the rest of the theatre for those who could afford it.

Shakespeare wrote exclusively for a theatre run by the Burbage family. James Burbage's theatre was called simply the Theatre, and was in Shoreditch, just outside the city of London. When the lease on the ground where it stood ran out in 1598, Burbage's two sons, Richard and Cuthbert, pulled off a risky and somewhat dubious coup. The landlord was threatening to pull down the building, so they got a group of friends together and dismantled the theatre without warning. They rowed the timber across the Thames and used it to build a new theatre on Bankside, which they called the Globe.

KEYWORDS

Groundlings: this was the term given to the people who paid only a penny and watched, standing, from the central arena in front of the stage.

Gallants: these people paid three pennies for the best gallery seats nearest the stage. Gallants were generally courtiers or nobility.

TODAY'S PERFORMANCE: "THE TEMPEST"

The Globe was a round theatre, as you might guess from the name, which Shakespeare referred to as a 'wooden O'. The chorus in *Henry V*, one of the first plays to be performed there, says:

> *Can this cockpit hold*
> *The vasty fields of France? Or may we cram*
> *Within this wooden O the very casques*
> *That did affright the air at Agincourt?*

All Elizabethan theatres of this kind followed a similar design.

* There were no moving sets – although there were plenty of props – but the back of the stage was hung with brightly coloured tapestries. Three doors at the back of the stage were the actors' entrances.

* Huge painted pillars supported the wooden canopy over the stage, which was decorated with the sun, moon and stars. Actors could be 'flown' in and out (in other words lowered and raised on ropes) through trapdoors in this ceiling.

* The area beneath the raised stage represented Hell, and trapdoors were used to raise or lower actors. The ghost of Hamlet's father speaks from beneath the stage; Hamlet actually says of him: '… you hear this fellow in the cellarage'.

Shakespeare owned a share in the Globe, and theatres were lucrative businesses. It was this, rather than his plays, that brought him most of his wealth. The theatre would be open from early autumn and through the winter. In the summer, London became hot and the plague could spread easily so the players – Shakespeare's company was called the Chamberlain's Men – would tour the country performing in schools, halls, market squares and on village greens.

One of the reasons the Globe was so successful was because it was the only theatre allowed to perform Shakespeare's plays, which were hugely popular. Shakespeare's career took off from the start and his work was widely admired; he quickly became recognized as the greatest play-wright and poet of the time.

Sadly, the Globe theatre did not last. In 1613, three years before Shakespeare's death, the Globe put on a performance of *Henry VIII*.

A piece of smouldering wadding from the stage cannon landed on the thatched roof and set fire to it. Within an hour, the theatre had burned to the ground, although amazingly all of the audience escaped unhurt.

THE STATUS OF THE THEATRE

When Shakespeare first began writing his plays, theatres were disapproved of and often banned by the authorities. This is why Bankside, just outside the city of London, became home to all sorts of entertainments banned within its walls. Bear-baiting arenas, brothels, theatres and inns all thrived, pulling crowds from the city. Bankside became a mildly disreputable playground for Londoners, and was inhabited by theatrical managers, actors and poets.

During Shakespeare's lifetime, the status of the theatre improved considerably. Although few well-to-do families would have gone so far as to encourage it as an ideal profession for their sons, theatres themselves became far more respectable, and Shakespeare's company performed in front of the Queen, Elizabeth I on many occasions.

KEY FACT There were already two theatres on Bankside when the Globe was built. The Rose had been built in 1587, and in 1594 the Swan opened. These would have had a similar layout to the Globe, with an open central area. They held around 3,000 people, larger than many of today's theatres. With no lighting, performances would be given in broad daylight, and there was no tradition of silence among the audience. They would chat, eat and drink – not to mention pickpocket – throughout the performance.

THE THEATRICAL LIFE

Theatre people worked extremely hard. They would often perform six different plays in a week, putting on an average of 17 new plays (and some old favourites, too) each season. They would perform in the afternoon, when it was light, leaving the mornings free to run around and do everything else. That meant making costumes and scenery and preparing for the afternoon's performance as well as rehearsing.

Everyone had to do a bit of everything, and Shakespeare acted as well as writing the plays. Richard Burbage played the leading roles, but

Shakespeare often took major parts. Time was so limited that the actors learned their lines alone in the evenings, and probably only rehearsed each new play together two or three times. In amongst all this, Shakespeare wrote nearly forty plays, often at an average rate of two a year. When you read or see his plays, it is worth bearing this in mind. It probably accounts for some of the inconsistencies or loopholes in the plot that you sometimes spot in the plays – they certainly seem forgivable under the circumstances.

Many of Shakespeare's plays give hints to the actors to remind them of their cues, since rehearsal time was so limited. Lines such as 'Who comes here?' are probably veiled cues to warn actors off stage that they are supposed to be entering now. Characters often signal their intent, too, with lines such as 'I'll away'. Again, the actor saying the line knows that they are supposed to leave the stage now.

Theatre companies were no place for women, and the whole company – usually about a dozen to fifteen men – would have taken all the parts. This may well be why a lot of Shakespeare's plays contain few parts for women, and probably also accounts for the fact that five of them contain leading female characters who spend much of the play dressed up as men. The Burbages' company would have included young men or boys who were well suited to playing female roles.

KEY FACT   Five of Shakespeare's leading women characters dress up as men for much of the play: Viola in *Twelfth Night*, Rosalind in *As You Like It*, Portia in *The Merchant of Venice*, Julia in *Two Gentlemen of Verona* and Imogen in *Cymbeline*.

* * * *SUMMARY * * * *

• Shakespeare wrote and performed at the Globe theatre on the south bank of the River Thames.

• During his lifetime, the theatre rose from being considered somewhat disreputable to being an acceptable profession.

• The actors all worked extremely hard, doing everything from making costumes and props to giving performances.

• There were no women in Elizabethan theatre companies, so all the female roles were taken by men.

Shakespeare's Language

Shakespeare's dialogue can be hard to follow nowadays, but he was using the everyday language of his time. Although, people didn't actually talk in verse, the vocabulary he used was nothing out of the ordinary. The problem for modern audiences is that we don't speak in the same way any more. Add to that the fact that much of the writing is in verse, and there is a great deal of imagery which needs (and deserves) to be thought about. But it's more than worth the effort and, once you get the hang of it, it becomes very easy to follow after all.

VOCABULARY AND GRAMMAR

Although Shakespeare's vocabulary was basically made up of words that were in common use at the time, he did have a huge vocabulary by any standards. He uses a total of over 17,000 different words in his plays and poems; an average well-educated person today generally has a vocabulary of around 4,000 words. The *Oxford English Dictionary* credits him with introducing almost 3,000 words into the language, although this simply means that his was the first recorded use of them – it doesn't mean he invented all of them.

This breadth of language is all the more remarkable when you realize that Shakespeare's education stopped at the age of 14, and that there were no dictionaries in those days (the first ever was compiled in 1604).

KEY FACT

Shakespeare's use of words was so accomplished that he used 7,000 words only once. To put this in perspective, the King James version of the Bible uses fewer than 7,000 individual words in total.

Grammar was taken less seriously in Shakespeare's day. That is to say that the rules of word order and sentence construction were much more flexible. The grammar schools of the time were so called because they taught Latin and Greek grammar, not English; Shakespeare probably never studied the grammar of his own language as a boy; indeed, it was over a century before books of English grammar were first produced. In Shakespeare's time, just as now, writing in verse also gave more scope for tweaking the order of words. But he probably knew more Latin and Greek than a top university classics graduate today.

VERSE AND PROSE

Shakespeare wrote chiefly in verse, and always used verse for the more serious, important speeches, in which more formal language was required. He did use prose, but mostly for more everyday conversations, and particularly for lower-class characters. In *A Midsummer Night's Dream*, for example, the noblemen and women generally speak in verse while the 'rude mechanicals' or workmen converse in prose.

Shakespeare's verse is almost always written in what is known as *iambic pentameter*. This type of verse has:

* ten beats, or syllables, to each line;
* alternating unstressed and stressed syllables (de-dúm de-dúm de-dúm de-dúm de-dúm).

The word *iambic* is a Greek word describing the pattern of stresses, or emphasis, in the line, and *pentameter* is a Latin word which means there are five pairs of stresses to each line. Here's an example of iambic pentameter from *Romeo and Juliet*, with the stressed syllables highlighted:

What's **in** a **name**? That **which** we **call** a **rose**
By **any oth**er **name** would **smell** as **sweet**

Shakespeare uses both rhyming and unrhymed iambic pentameter. These are known as either rhyming verse or, when the verse doesn't rhyme, blank verse.

There are some varations on standard iambic pentameter which Shakespeare uses, and which are worth knowing about:

Feminine ending

This term describes a line that has an extra, eleventh beat at the end. This beat is unstressed. Feminine endings give the verse a ponderous feel, especially when several are used together:

> To **be**, or **not** to **be**: that **is** the **quest**ion:
> Whe**ther** 'tis **nob**ler **in** the **mind** to **suff**er
> The **slings** and **arr**ows of out**rage**ous **for**tune,
> Or **to** take **arms** a**gainst** a **sea** of **troub**les...

Caesura

This describes a break within a line created by punctuation. If you look at the quotation above, from Hamlet's famous speech, you can see that in the first line there are two of these – a comma and a colon – indicating pauses in the delivery of the line.

Run-on lines

These are lines that have no punctuation at the end of them, indicating that the sense of the line runs on to the following line. The second and third lines of the quotation from *Hamlet* illustrate this, and the lines should be run smoothly together.

KEY FACT

Shakespeare's actors would have had little time to rehearse. What's more, they would not have had a copy of the whole play, only the scenes they were in. Even then, there wasn't time to write out long speeches for everyone's copy of the script, only for the person giving the speech. So your copy of the script would have contained little beyond your lines and your cue lines from the other actors. Not a lot to go on, really.

Clues in the way the lines were phrased and punctuated would have been a big help to the actors. These 'codes' would have given tips on how to perform the lines in much the same way that a director coaches actors today.

Run-on lines add speed to a speech, while caesuras slow them down. Lines to be read at an average pace simply have punctuation at the end of the line. Bearing this in mind, you can see how the *Hamlet* speech above varies in pace. As Hamlet ponders, the lines are very broken, but each time he grasps a train of thought they run together as his thoughts run away with him, and then slow down again. Look how the next few lines go, noticing the punctuation:

> *Or to take arms against a sea of troubles,*
> *And by opposing end them? To die: to sleep;*
> *No more; and, by a sleep to say we end*
> *The heart-ache and the thousand natural shocks*
> *That flesh is heir to, 'tis a consummation*
> *Devoutly to be wish'd. To die, to sleep;*
> *To sleep: perchance to dream: ay, there's the rub;*
> *For in that sleep of death what dreams may come*
> *When we have shuffled off this mortal coil,*
> *Must give us pause.*

This should illustrate one of the many reasons why seeing Shakespeare's plays performed is so much closer to the original intention than simply reading them. If you read the plays, you have to take note of the pattern and punctuation of the lines to grasp fully how Shakespeare intended them to sound.

PUNCTUATION AND SPELLING

It is worth mentioning pronunciation here, which was not always the same as it is now. Often, knowing how the lines should scan helps you to work out the punctuation. The most significant difference here between Shakespeare's time and today is words which end **-ed**. This was usually pronounced as a separate syllable, so that 'wished' would be pronounced 'wishèd'. This of course affects the way the lines scan. If Shakespeare didn't want the final syllable stressed, this is often indicated with an apostrophe, as in the passage above: 'wish'd'.

Spelling was not standardized in Shakespeare's day (he even spelt his own name in several different ways), and the spellings you find in texts of his work are not necessarily his own. We don't have any of the original working scripts of the plays (which would mostly have been just the actors parts written out); what we have are the earliest published versions, many of which were not printed, in the **First Folio** edition, until 1623, seven years after Shakespeare's death. Many subsequent editions have 'corrected' spellings so that it is impossible to be sure of the original version.

KEYWORD

First Folio: First Folio The first collected works of Shakespeare. The word folio refers to the way the printer folded the paper on which he printed the book, ready for binding. Folio pages are folded once to make two leaves, or four sides, of paper. Quarto pages were folded twice to produce four leaves, or eight sides (which were then cut). There are other folio and quarto editions of Shakespeare's plays. Some of the different versions of certain plays vary widely from each other.

IMAGERY

Perhaps Shakespeare's greatest talent lay in his ability to use beautiful and apt imagery to describe ideas and objects. He employed all sorts of linguistic techniques, such as metaphors and similes, to give colour and feeling to his words. Metaphors and similes are descriptions that are apt but not literal. To give you an example, here are a few of the ways Shakespeare uses imagery.

* 'The moon looks with a watery eye.' (*A Midsummer Night's Dream*).

* 'Tis now the very witching time of night, When churchyards yawn and hell itself breathes out Contagion to this world.' (*Hamlet*).

* 'If music be the food of love...' (*Twelfth Night*).

* 'Sleep that knits up the ravelled sleeve of care...' (*Macbeth*).

* 'I am constant as the northern star' (*Julius Caesar*).

Shakespeare often paints a scene with the most moving images and extended metaphors. From *Romeo and Juliet*, here is Juliet willing it to be night time, when her new, secret husband Romeo will come to her:

...Come civil night,
Thou sober-suited matron all in black,
And learn me how to lose a winning match,
Play'd for a pair of stainless maidenhoods...

Come night, come Romeo, come thou day in night,
For thou wilt lie upon the wings of night,
Whiter than new snow upon a raven's back:
Come gentle night, come loving black-brow'd night,
Give me my Romeo...

THE DEVELOPMENT OF SHAKESPEARE'S STYLE

Shakespeare's early works differ widely from his later ones. He was writing for over twenty years, so it's hardly surprising that his style developed during that time. Audiences expect what they are given, and writers provide what the audience seems to want. It takes time to adapt your style and take the audience along with you, rather than alienate them.

When Shakespeare began writing, audiences expected simple, straightforward plays, with characters who used grand language, full of **rhetoric**, and made lots of long speeches. They also expected characters to speak in rhyming verse. Marlowe had gone a little way towards breaking down this convention, using blank verse from time to time, but Shakespeare had little choice but to write in this style too.

> **KEYWORD**
>
> Rhetoric: stylish, clever, formal speech designed to sound effective, often incorporating references to mythology or literature.

To begin with, Shakespeare discovered he had a talent for being clever and witty with words, and he loved to play with them. This lent itself better to comedy than to tragedy in many ways; the fashion was for clever, witty, quick dialogue in comedy, with the humour often accentuated by the rhythm of the lines. Some of his early tragic plays could be a little heavy-handed and sentimental in places. The description of the death of the princes in the tower in *Richard III* is an example of this.

As Shakespeare's experience grew, his use of language grew with it. By the mid to late 1590s, his serious and even tragic dialogue was arguably better than his comedy. He was starting to take more liberties with the traditional rhythmic, rhyming style, which freed him to be more honest and realistic about the emotions he was describing. He also abandoned his earlier tendency to be clever for the sake of it, with speeches which were intricately worded but overlong, and added little if anything to the drama.

By about 1600, Shakespeare had become a true master of his art, and most of his greatest plays were written around or after this date, including *Julius Caesar, Hamlet, King Lear, Othello* and *Macbeth* and the great comedies *Twelfth Night* and *As You Like It*. In the earlier plays, for example, soliloquies are generally used to impart information or to recite an inward-looking piece of verse, but the later plays employ the technique to give real insight into the mind, the thinking and often the indecision of the character.

As time went on, Shakespeare's style became freer, and his imagery more complex. *King Lear* is one of the best examples of this. Many of the later plays show a greater fascination with human nature than with detailed plot: *King Lear, Antony and Cleopatra, Measure for Measure* and *The Winter's Tale*, for example.

In around 1611, Shakespeare wrote what some critics consider his finest play, *The Tempest*. This play, very nearly his last, stretches the language and form of seventeenth-century drama to its greatest limit. It is mostly written in a very free form of blank verse, using imagery which is perfectly apt, and describing thoughts in a way that is complex but not obscure. If you compare it with an early work, such as *Richard III*, you will see how far Shakespeare's style travelled during the course of his career.

✳✳✳SUMMARY✳✳✳

● Shakespeare uses verse for serious and important speech, and prose for everyday speech and for lower-class characters.

● Shakespeare's style of verse is known as *iambic pentameter*, it has ten beats to a line, alternating stressed and unstressed syllables.

● The punctuation and spelling you see in editions of Shakespeare's plays are not necessarily his own.

● Shakespeare's earlier plays follow a fairly rigid format, but as he developed he began to play around with accepted patterns of verse and rhyme, and to use increasingly complex imagery.

An Introduction to the Plays

Shakespeare wrote nearly forty plays, on an impressive range of subjects. There were historical plays, comedies and tragedies, **dark comedies** and plays on classical themes, such as *Julius Caesar* and *Timon of Athens*. The stories he told were rarely his own, and he never pretended they were. He was retelling old tales.

THE MAIN SOURCES
Shakespeare used all sorts of sources for the plots and stories of his plays, from classical to contemporary writings. In some cases we know a lot about the sources he used, in others we have no idea where the story came from. He had certain favourite writers and books to which he referred, however. His chief sources for the history plays were the chroniclers of his time and of the previous two or three centuries:

KEYWORD

Dark comedy: a term first coined by H.B. Charlton in *Shakespearean Comedy* (1938), he argued that the term 'problem plays' also used to describe them was too loose as in a sense 'all plays are problem plays'. Essentially a play that is sombre in tone, but that has a happy ending; too serious to be a comedy, but not tragic enough to be a tragedy. Shakespeare's dark comedies include *Measure for Measure, Troilus and Cressida* and *All's Well That Ends Well.*

Raphael Holinshed
He was a near contemporary of Shakespeare (Holinshed died around 1580), who recorded the history of England, Scotland and Ireland in an account commonly known as *Holinshed's Chronicles*. Shakespeare used these as a main source for many of his historical plays, although he often embellished or adapted them. For example, in *Richard II* he alters the character of John of Gaunt, to turn him from a greedy empire-builder to a wise and patriotic nobleman. This was probably because Elizabeth I was a direct descendant of John of Gaunt. Holinshed was his main source for *Richard II, Richard III, Henry IV Parts I and II, Henry V, Henry VI Parts I, II and III* and *Henry VIII*. This last play, *Henry VIII*, is unusual in that it is the only play for which Shakespeare

made no dramatic alterations to the story at all, but related it almost exactly as it was in his source, with the characters' personalities intact. Some people even think, because of this, that it wasn't written by Shakespeare at all, although there is no other evidence to support this.

Jean Froissart

Another chronicler, Froissart lived in the second half of the fourteenth century. He was French, but travelled widely in England, Scotland, and Italy, and wrote about European history from 1325 to 1400, covering the reigns of Edward III and Richard II. He was a main source for *Richard II*.

Samuel Daniel

Almost exactly the same age as Shakespeare, Daniel was a poet, dramatist and courtier. In1595 he wrote the epic poem *A History of the Civil Wars Between York and Lancaster*. About two years later, Shakespeare used this as one of his sources for *Henry IV Parts I and II*.

Edward Hall

Hall was a historian who lived in the first half of the sixteenth century and wrote *The Union of the Noble Families of York and Lancaster*. Shakespeare drew on *Hall's Chronicle* (as it is generally known), to write *Henry VI Parts I, II and III*, and *Henry VIII*.

Shakespeare used a much wider range of sources for the plots of his comedies, some of which he stuck to quite closely and others of which he adapted widely. Sometimes he combined two or more plots from different writers.

Giovanni Boccacio

Shakespeare's most important source, Giovanni Boccaccio was an Italian writer who lived in the fourteenth century. Boccaccio wrote stories in verse and prose and these were generally medieval romances; Chaucer translated some of his works, as did others. Shakespeare may have read Boccaccio's work in the original Italian, but he probably often worked from translations. Boccaccio's greatest collection of stories was the *Decameron*, which he completed in 1358. This was one of Shakespeare's key sources, which he drew on for *All's Well That Ends Well*, *Cymbeline* and *The Two Gentlemen of Verona*.

KEY FACT There is no known source for three of Shakespeare's comedies: *Love's Labour's Lost*, *A Midsummer Night's Dream* and *The Tempest*. Although we can't be certain, it is generally assumed that the plots of these plays were Shakespeare's own invention.

There are several sources that Shakespeare used for only a single one of his comedies, or upon which he might have drawn for a particular character or a single turn of plot. One of the writers he used was Plautus, a Roman dramatist who lived around 200 BC, and who wrote over twenty comedies, as well as revising as many as a hundred or so works written by earlier playwrights. His play, *The Menaechmi*, was the basis for Shakespeare's *The Comedy of Errors*, although Shakespeare adapted the plot by adding a second set of twins to increase the comic confusion.

Shakespeare also used the classical writers Plutarch and Ovid as minor sources for his comedies. Geoffrey Chaucer, who lived about two hundred years before Shakespeare, was another important source.

Shakespeare's tragedies also drew on a number of writers for their origins. Among the most important of these were:

Plutarch
A Greek historian, biographer and philosopher, Plutarch lived around AD 100. His biographical work *Parallel Lives* pairs up biographies of 23 great politicians and soldiers of ancient Greece with 23 biographies of great Roman leaders. Shakespeare used this as his main source for his Roman plays: *Antony and Cleopatra*; *Coriolanus*; *Julius Caesar* and *Timon of Athens*.

Raphael Holinshed

Holinshed's *Chronicles* covered early English and Scottish history, much of which was little more than legend. These early histories provided the inspiration for *King Lear*, *Macbeth* and *Cymbeline*, although he also drew on other sources for details, sub-plots and other characters in these plays. The story of Lear was well known, and Shakespeare almost certainly drew on Edmund Spenser's version of it in *The Faerie Queen*, the famous poem published in 1590.

Saxo Grammaticus

This Danish chronicler lived around AD 1200, and wrote *Gesta Danorum* (in Latin), an account of the legendary and historical kings of Denmark. (Guess which play this was a source for.) He tells the story of Amleth, whose father the king is murdered by his own brother, who then marries his widow. Amleth is frightened and pretends to be mad to avoid being murdered.

Cinthio

This Italian author wrote the *Hecatommithi*, a novel which was the main source for *Othello*.

Arthur Brooke

Another writer Shakespeare used only once, but for one of his major plays. Brooke wrote a poem in 1562 entitled *The Tragical History of Romeus and Juliet*. This was not the only source for *Romeo and Juliet*, since there were other versions of the story around, but it was certainly the main one.

THE CHRONOLOGY OF THE PLAYS

Shakespeare's style developed considerably during his career, as we have already seen. The subject matter also changed to some extent: most of the comedies were early, along with the histories, while the great tragedies came later.

It is very difficult, and at times impossible, to date Shakespeare's plays accurately, because the first performances are not recorded. There are four main sources of information for working out the order in which the plays were written.

✳ Some plays refer to historical events or scientific discoveries, which help to date them. For example, in *Twelfth Night* Maria says of Malvolio that 'he does smile his face into more lines, than is in the new map, with the augmentation of the Indies'. This map, covered in lines indicating comparative distances, first appeared in 1600.

✳ There are some records of performances taken from contemporary diaries written by people who attended them.

✳ In some cases, the source of the play was published during Shakespeare's life; his version must have followed this.

✳ The plays obviously preceded the first time they appeared in print, which many of them did during Shakespeare's life.

KEY FACT

Shakespeare had to write plays that fitted the actors in the pemanent company for which he was writing. It was no good writing a part for which there was no suitable performer. This tells us something about his fellow actors. For example, Will Kempe, the resident actor who played clowns, was a bit of a buffoon. He played the Nurse's man, Peter, in *Romeo and Juliet*. Shakespeare also wrote Dogberry in *Much Ado About Nothing* for him. When he left the company in 1600, he was replaced by Robert Armin, a much more reflective, sophisticated comic. Shakespeare wrote Touchstone (*As You Like It*), Feste (*Twelfth Night*) and the Fool (*King Lear*) for him.

Shakespeare's plays can therefore be dated with relative accuracy, and placed in a rough order in which they were first performed – and they would have been performed as soon as they were completed. Although the development of Shakespeare's style cannot be used to date the plays conclusively, it supports the accepted chronology. So here is a list of the plays in the approximate order in which they were written:

First performed	Play	First performed	Play
1590–1591	Henry VI part II	1599–1600	Twelfth Night
1590–1591	Henry VI part III	1600–1601	Hamlet
1591–1592	Henry VI part I	1600–1601	The Merry Wives of Windsor
1592–1593	Richard III	1601–1602	Troilus and Cressida
1592–1593	The Comedy of Errors	1602–1603	All's Well That Ends Well
1593–1594	Titus Andronicus	1604–1605	Measure for Measure
1593–1594	The Taming of the Shrew	1604–1605	Othello
1594–1595	The Two Gentlemen of Verona	1605–1606	King Lear
1594–1595	Love's Labour's Lost	1605–1606	Macbeth
1594–1595	Romeo and Juliet	1606–1607	Antony and Cleopatra
1595–1596	Richard II	1607–1608	Coriolanus
1595–1596	A Midsummer Night's Dream	1607–1608	Timon of Athens
1596–1597	King John	1608–1609	Pericles
1596–1597	The Merchant of Venice	1609–1610	Cymbeline
1597–1598	Henry IV part I	1610–1611	The Winter's Tale
1597–1598	Henry IV part II	1611–1612	The Tempest
1598–1599	Much Ado About Nothing	1612–1613	Henry VIII
1598–1599	Henry V	1612–1613	The Two Noble Kinsmen
1599–1600	Julius Caesar		
1599–1600	As You Like It		

QUARTOS AND FOLIOS

The first collected edition of Shakespeare's plays was the First Folio, put together in 1623. (Actually one of the plays, *Pericles*, was omitted, as was *The Two Noble Kinsmen*, which Shakespeare is now thought to have co-written.) The First Folio is a kind of 'official' version of the plays, printed on large sheets of paper.

The quartos are smaller-format editions of single plays. Eighteen of the plays exist in quartos, which were published during Shakespeare's lifetime. However, we don't really know how the printers got hold of the material; some of the quartos seem to have been pirated. There are certainly pirated quartos of *Hamlet, Romeo and Juliet, Henry V* and *The Merry Wives of Windsor*. The other quartos may well not have been officially sanctioned versions either. Some of them are pretty accurate, some far from accurate (relative to the First Folio, that is).

Sometimes there are several versions of a play. For example:

* the first quarto of *Hamlet* was the pirated version which came out in 1603;

* this was followed in 1604 by the second quarto, which was probably taken from Shakespeare's own manuscript (none of the original manuscripts of any of Shakespeare's works survive);

* the First Folio edition of *Hamlet* came out in 1623.

In putting together a modern version of the plays, editors have had to decide which version to work from. Often they have taken parts from two or more versions. They have also had to compare versions to sort out confusion over certain words or lines, where they are unreadable in one version, or where the printer may have misread the manuscript. To give you an example, the word 'five' would have been written in Elizabethan handwriting as *fiue*. This might easily have been misread as *fine* or *fume* by the printer.

A PLAY IN FIVE ACTS

You'll notice when you read Shakespeare's plays that they are divided into five acts. However, there are no scene divisions and very few act divisions in the original versions. These versions do not give place headings at the beginning of scenes, such as 'A clearing in the forest', and stage directions are very scarce.

All these things have been added by later editors of the plays, to make them fit into the format of their own times. Editors started to make these changes in the eighteenth century, although plenty of changes were made later, particularly during the nineteenth century. Editors have often tampered with punctuation as well, on the basis that the Elizabethans were illiterate and probably got it wrong. Modern scholars disagree with this and reckon that the punctuation, while probably not

Shakespeare's own, would have been added by his contemporaries who knew what they were doing. The punctuation may well have been a clue as to how to deliver the lines, as we saw earlier.

＊＊＊＊SUMMARY ＊＊＊＊

● Shakespeare drew on lots of different sources for the plots of his plays – classical authors, historians and story writers.

● No one knows exactly when all the plays were first produced, but there is an approximate chronology. Most of the histories and comedies were written in the first half of Shakespeare's career; he wrote the great tragedies later.

● The most reliable version of Shakespeare's plays is the First Folio, published seven years after his death. No one knows quite where the quartos – printed during his lifetime – originated, but many were dubious and some certainly pirated.

● Later editors, particularly in the Eighteenth and Nineteenth centuries, have changed the original punctuation and added scene breaks and stage directions, and divided up the plays into acts.

The Comedies

A MIDSUMMER NIGHT'S DREAM

This play really does have a wonderful dreamlike quality, and at the end the human characters are not sure whether the events of the night (it all takes place in one night) have really happened or were simply a dream. The play is almost entirely set in a wood near Athens which, for the night in question, is very much the fairies' domain.

A Midsummer Night's Dream was written in about 1595, almost certainly for a special performance at a wedding – which accounts for the plot revolving around the wedding of the Duke of Athens, Theseus, to Hippolyta. This is the first of Shakespeare's great comedies, and one of the most popular. It is interesting to compare this play with *The Tempest* which was written about 16 years later, but is also a dreamlike play about magic and enchantments; in some ways it is like *A Midsummer Night's Dream* for grown-ups.

KEY CHARACTERS

Oberon and Titania King and Queen of the fairies. Much of the plot stems from these two falling out over a changeling boy (half human, half fairy) whom they each want to have as a pageboy.

Puck Oberon's good-hearted but mischievous fairy servant. He was a traditional character out of fairy stories who played tricks on village folk, such as turning milk sour.

The young lovers Various love triangles go on between the lovers, which are resolved at the end of the play. The women – Helena and Hermia – are better drawn characters than the men – Demetrius and Lysander – who are Shakespeare's examples of typically foolish men in love.

Bottom The chief 'rude mechanical', who is a large and exuberant character.

The story

On the eve of the wedding of the Duke of Athens, four lovers – all noblemen and women – find themselves in a wood near the city. So too do a group of workmen, the 'rude mechanicals' (Elizabethan-speak for humble tradesmen), who have come to rehearse a play they hope to perform at the wedding in honour of the Duke. All of these humans get caught up in the activities of the fairies, and there are lots of enchantments and love potions, with disastrous and comical results. In the end, however, everything is resolved satisfactorily, and the rude mechanicals' play is performed (a 'play within a play').

KEY QUOTATIONS

✳ Oberon's greeting to Titania:
   Ill-met by moonlight, proud Titania...

✳ Puck describing the place where Titania sleeps:
   I know a bank whereon the wild thyme blows,
   Where oxlips and the nodding violet grows...

✳ Puck's epilogue:
   If we shadows have offended,
   Think but this, and all is mended:
   That you have but slumbered here,
   While these visions did appear.

AS YOU LIKE IT

This play is mostly set in the Forest of Arden, not far from Shakespeare's home town of Stratford-upon-Avon. It is Shakespeare's greatest illustration of the rural idyll, with its lessons about how beautiful life can be away from the formality and pomp of civic and court life. Many people regard this play as the greatest work of English literature on the pastoral theme, which was very popular at the time it was written.

Shakespeare takes the pastoral ideal as the setting for a romantic story. However, he avoids sentimentalism largely by adding a character who does not appear in his key source, *Rosalynde* (1590) by Thomas Lodge. The melancholy but likeable Jacques (pronounced 'Jay-quiz') is there to cast a cynical eye on love and successfully keeps any sugary romanticism out of the play.

KEY CHARACTERS

Rosalind The banished niece of Duke Frederick, Rosalind dresses as a young man when she enters the forest. She is in love with Orlando and, dressed as a man, flirts with him without giving away her identity.

Celia Duke Frederick's daughter. She flees to the forest with her cousin Rosalind, where she meets and falls in love with Oliver.

Orlando Also in the forest after being banished, Orlando is in love with Rosalind and pours out his heart to her when she is in disguise, without realizing who she is.

Oliver Orlando's elder brother, this villain undergoes a conversion after Orlando rescues him from a lion, and falls in love with Celia.

Jacques A follower of the banished Duke (not to be confused with Duke Frederick), he is melancholy and wise.

Touchstone The court jester, he accompanies Rosalind and Celia to the forest.

The story

Duke Frederick banishes both Rosalind and (separately) Orlando, who both flee to the Forest of Arden. Once there, they find that Rosalind's father – previously banished – is also there. The play revolves around the pastoral life of the forest, and centres on Rosalind, dressed as a man, persuading Orlando to woo her 'as if I were your very, very Rosalind'.

Rosalind's bright, charming and witty personality is what drives the play along. Eventually things are resolved and everyone is allowed back home, true identities are revealed and all ends happily. In a break with tradition, a woman, Rosalind, delivers the epilogue that ends the play.

KEY QUOTATIONS

✳ Jacques on the seven ages of man:

> *All the world's a stage;*
> *And all the men and women merely players:*
> *They have their exits and their entrances...*

✳ Rosalind to Orlando:

> *Men are April when they woo, December when they wed; maids are*
> *May when they are maids, but the sky changes when they are wives.*

LOVE'S LABOUR'S LOST

This is one of Shakespeare's earlier comedies, and is sometimes considered to be a little heavy-handed in some ways. For example, it contains a long speech by one of the leading characters, Berowne, on the advantages of barbarism. It is a delightful speech, but the whole plot seems to stand still for it. In Shakespeare's later plays he learned not to write long, clever speeches which added nothing to the play, but to make them pertinent to the plot. However, the play is still entertaining and well worth getting to know. The courtier Berowne, and the object of his affections, Rosaline, are the wittiest and strongest characters, and very reminiscent of Benedict and Beatrice in Shakespeare's later play, *Much Ado About Nothing*.

The story

The play is about the King of Navarre and his three close friends, Berowne, Dumaine and Longaville. The King persuades them all to join him in a pledge to spend the next three years studying: to eat only one meal a day, to fast one day a week, to sleep only three hours a night and – here's the crunch – not to see a woman for all that time. But their oath is jeopardized when the Princess of France pays a state visit with her three ladies-in-waiting: Rosaline, Katharine and Maria.

The men immediately fall in love, and much secret letter-sending follows. Letters get muddled up, tricks are played on unsuspecting lovers and, of course, they all discover the truth in the end. The play ends with the four pairs of lovers betrothed to be married in a year's time.

MUCH ADO ABOUT NOTHING

There are only two specifically recorded performances of this play during Shakespeare's lifetime; on one of these occasions it was entitled *Benedick and Beatrice*, after two of the main characters. The plot of the play really revolves around the other characters, but it is these two who have the greatest appeal with their quick, barbed exchanges of repartee, and Shakespeare clearly intended them to dominate.

The sub-plot in which others scheme to bring the sparring Beatrice and Benedick together is Shakespeare at his best comedy-writing form. The central plot is more like a tragedy than a comedy, however, except that the conclusion is happy. In the less tragic moments, the sophisticated comedy of Beatrice and Benedick is offset by the basic humour of the local constable, sexton and watchmen.

KEY CHARACTERS

Don Pedro Prince of Arragon.

Don John his illegitimate half-brother, who is bitter against Don Pedro and causes all the trouble.

Leonato Governor of Messina.

Hero Leonato's daughter.

Beatrice Hero's cousin and close friend.

Benedick A companion of Don Pedro, who falls in love with Beatrice.

Claudio Another companion of Don Pedro, who falls in love with Hero.

Dogberry A constable.

The story
Claudio falls in love with Hero and they are engaged to be married. But Don John, jealous of Claudio, wrecks the wedding by claiming that Hero has been unfaithful, and providing false evidence. Hero faints, and her family then pretends she is dead until things are resolved. This casts a heavy atmosphere over the whole play for a while, but eventually Don John's wickedness is discovered and Hero reappears.

THE COMEDY OF ERRORS
This is probably Shakespeare's first comedy, and it is also his shortest play. Although it lacks some of the subtlety, maturity and depth of many of his later comedies, it is a well structured, slick and very funny farce.

KEY CHARACTERS

Egeon A merchant from Syracuse.

Aemilia His wife, now an abbess at Ephesus.

Antipholus of Ephesus and **Antipholus of Syracuse** Identical twin brothers, sons to Egeon and Aemilia.

Dromio of Ephesus and **Dromio of Syracuse** Identical twin brothers, servants each to one Antipholus.

Adriana Wife of Antipholus of Ephesus.

Luciana Her sister.

The story

This is a story of two pairs of twins separated shortly after birth, when a shipwreck splits up the family. The mother, Aemilia, believes all her family lost or dead, and has become an abbess. The others all know of the existence of some but not other members of their family. Each Dromio twin has remained as servant to one of the Antipholus twins. The play is, as the title suggests, a series of errors based on mistaken identity, which becomes so contorted it is hard to follow until the final scene, when all the loose ends are tied up.

THE MERCHANT OF VENICE

This play is often seen as a racist condemnation of Jews in their not uncommon role of money-lenders, and many modern productions of it seem to highlight this aspect in the light of modern racial attitudes making the play out to be extreme in the racism. But Shakespeare is more subtle than this, and the conflict between Jew and Christian is more evenly balanced in this play.

Shylock the Jew is not painted as a representation of evil, but as a man who has been despised simply for being a Jew. His response to this has been to become so embittered that he has grown into the heartless and inhuman person that his enemies have painted him as. His daughter Jessica, however, is also a Jew but is a sympathetic character.

KEY CHARACTERS

Shylock A Jewish moneylender who hates Antonio for his attitude to him and for under-cutting him in business.

Bassanio A gentleman who is a suitor to Portia.

Antonio Bassanio's wealthy friend, who borrows money from Shylock on Bassanio's behalf.

Portia A rich and beautiful young woman whose father deemed in his will that she must marry the man who solves the riddle of the three caskets he has prepared, and chooses the right one.

Lorenzo A young man in love with Jessica who eventually marries her.

Jessica Shylock's daughter, who elopes taking a casket of jewels and money of her father's.

The story

Antonio borrows money from Shylock to lend to Bassanio so that he can woo Portia. Shylock agrees to the loan on condition that if the debt is not repaid, Antonio will let Shylock take a pound of flesh instead. Antonio does find he is unable to pay, and Shylock takes him to court to exact his recompense. Portia, however, turns up disguised as a man and presents herself (or himself) as a lawyer. She spots a loophole in the law that everyone else has missed, and the case is resolved in Antonio's favour.

KEY QUOTATIONS

✻ Shylock justifying his revenge:

I am a Jew. Hath not a Jew eyes? Hath not a Jew hands,
organs, dimensions, senses, affections, passions?…if you prick
us, do we not bleed? if you tickle us, do we not laugh? if you
poison us, do we not die? And if you wrong us, shall we not
revenge? If we are like you in the rest, we will resemble you in that.

✻ Portia pleading for mercy:

The quality of mercy is not strain'd,
It droppeth as the gentle rain from heaven
Upon the place beneath: it is twice bless'd;
It blesses him that gives, and him that takes…

THE MERRY WIVES OF WINDSOR

This is one of Shakespeare's later comedies, written in about 1600. It is commonly thought, although not certain, that Queen Elizabeth so enjoyed the character of Falstaff in *Henry IV Parts I and II* that she asked Shakespeare to write one more play about him that showed him in love. It is a thoroughly enjoyable farce which takes the central character out of the warlike court of the King in *Henry VI* and sets him in middle-class Windsor. Instead of making fun of everyone else, he becomes the butt of the joke himself.

The story

Sir John Falstaff turns fortune-hunter, not by pursuing widows but by setting himself up as the soldier-lover of married women who have access to their husbands' purses. However, the two women he chooses to woo – Mistress Page and Mistress Ford – are more than a match for him. They lead him a merry dance, playing tricks which leave him cudgelled, tossed into the freezing River Thames and subjected to all sorts of indignities, before he eventually realizes that they have been playing with him.

THE TAMING OF THE SHREW

The biggest difficulty with this play is that it is so politically incorrect by modern standards that it is hard to see it through Elizabethan eyes. The story of a man taking a shrewish young woman and turning her into a docile and obedient wife sticks in the throat somewhat. But if you can disregard this aspect of the play, it is a terrific romp, and Katharine and Petruchio make a great pair of sparring partners. It is one of Shakespeare's early plays, and not one of the great comedies, but well worth watching or reading.

The story

Baptista has two daughters. The younger daughter, Bianca, is beautiful and mild-mannered, and has lots of suitors, while her elder sister, Katharine, has a foul temper. Baptista can see that it is going to be pretty hard to marry off Katharine, so he announces to Bianca's suitors that he won't allow her to be married until her older sister has a husband.

KEY CHARACTERS

Baptista A fabulously wealthy gentleman of Padua.

Katharine His eldest daughter, cursed with a foul temper.

Bianca His sweet and charming younger daughter.

Petruchio Katharine's suitor and then husband.

Lucentio One of Bianca's suitors, who finally marries her.

Gremio and Hortensio Unsuccessful suitors for Bianca.

One of Bianca's suitors tells his friend, Petruchio, about this, and he declares that he would happily marry anyone as rich as Katharine, whatever her temper. So he sets out on his mission to 'tame the shrew', and in the process falls in love with her. Meanwhile, Bianca's suitors are using various ruses and disguises to woo her. By the end of the play, Katharine is the most obedient wife of all.

KEY QUOTATION

＊ Petruchio to Katharine, at the end of the play:

   Why there's a wench. Come on and kiss me Kate.

THE TEMPEST

This is one of Shakespeare's very last plays, and many argue that it is his greatest. It is impossible to state objectively which is really the greatest play, but *The Tempest* is undoubtedly up there with *Hamlet*, *Macbeth*, *Othello* and *King Lear* as a key contender. It has an extraordinary atmosphere of magic and enchantment, and the language is Shakespeare at his best.

Prospero is an enigmatic ruler of his island, and he and his spirits are more clearly drawn characters than the ordinary mortals, drawing the audience in to their world. The relationship between Prospero and Ariel is the most complex in the play.

KEY CHARACTERS

Prospero A magician, the deposed Duke of Milan.

Miranda His daughter.

Ariel A spirit, Prospero's servant.

Caliban A monster, Prospero's slave.

Antonio Prospero's brother, who deposed him.

Alonzo King of Naples.

Ferdinand His son.

Stephano and **Trinculo** The butler and court jester, who provide the humour in the play.

The story

An enchanted island, somewhere in the Mediterranean, is inhabited by the magician Prospero, his daughter Miranda, and the two creatures he controls: Ariel, a spirit of the air, and Caliban, who is half human, half monster. At the start of the play, Prospero conjures up a huge tempest so that his brother, Antonio, who long ago seized the dukedom that was rightfully Prospero's, is shipwrecked on the island along with the King of Naples, the King's brother and his son, Ferdinand. A few lords and two crew members are also washed up on the island.

Prospero uses his powers to punish those who have done him wrong, sending Ariel to enchant them. Through Ariel, he controls their movements throughout the play until, at the end, he brings them all together. He forgives his enemies, gives Miranda to be married to Ferdinand, and reclaims his dukedom. Finally, he gives up his magic book and staff, and sets Ariel free.

KEY QUOTATIONS

✳ Prospero, on giving up magic to return to Milan:
> …I'll break my staff,
> Bury it certain fathoms in the earth,
> And deeper than did ever plummet sound
> I'll drown my book.

✳ Miranda, on discovering men for the first time in her life:
> O brave new world, That has such people in't!

✳ Prospero:
> Our revels now are ended. These our actors,
> As I foretold you, were all spirits, and
> Are melted into air, into thin air;
> …We are such stuff
> As dreams are made on; and our little life
> Is rounded with a sleep.

THE TWO GENTLEMEN OF VERONA

This is one of Shakespeare's first four comedies, sometimes known as his experimental comedies (the other three are *A Comedy of Errors*, *The Taming of the Shrew* and *Love's Labour's Lost*. Each of them takes a different type of theme, in a way which suggests that Shakespeare was deliberately trying to extend his range. In *The Two Gentlemen of Verona*, he seems to be using the genre of material classed as Romance: the poetic approach to romantic love which was popular at the time.

However, the general verdict is that, while his later comedies were prime examples of this style, *The Two Gentlemen of Verona* isn't. It is clearly the work of a great writer – and it is thoroughly entertaining – but it is not regarded as one of his great works.

The story

Proteus and Valentine are close friends, both living in Verona. When Proteus falls in love with Julia, his company becomes a little tedious, so Valentine goes travelling and Proteus elects to stay behind. But his father sends him off to join Valentine in Milan, where Valentine has by now fallen in love with Sylvia. However, as soon as Proteus sees Sylvia, he too falls in love with her, and plots to steal her from his friend. Julia then follows Proteus to Milan disguised as a boy, and finds out what is going on. After much appalling behaviour by Proteus, everything is resolved and everyone (rather generously) forgives Proteus absolutely.

TWELFTH NIGHT

Twelfth Night is generally regarded as one of Shakespeare's finest comedies. It is named after the feast that marks the end of Christmas. In Shakespeare's time this celebration would have recalled the Roman celebration, the Feast of Fools, and other medieval style antics, which entailed masquerades and carnival revels. Many of these activities involved inverting the normal world; the Lord of Misrule was a fool set up as lord to show up how foolish the lords really were. *Twelfth Night* is largely about delusion, and – in the character of Malvolio – about bringing down those who have become full of their own importance.

KEY CHARACTERS

Viola One of Shakespeare's most charming heroines, who dresses as a boy after she is shipwrecked.

Sebastian Viola's brother.

Orsino The Duke, who is in love with Olivia.

Olivia A beautiful countess, who is in mourning for her brother.

Feste Olivia's jester.

Malvolio Olivia's vain and pompous steward.

Sir Toby Belch Olivia's uncle, chief persecutor of Malvolio and a lovable rogue.

The character of Feste, one of Shakespeare's great fools, has echoes of a Lord of Misrule. Although he is a fool, he is often the wisest character in the play, and seems to be the only one perceptive enough to suspect Viola's true identity, although he never overtly challenges it.

The story

Twin brother and sister Sebastian and Viola are shipwrecked on the coast of Illyria and separated, each believing the other drowned. Viola disguises herself as a boy, Cesario. She becomes page to the Duke Orsino, with whom she falls in love. But he sends her to woo Olivia for him – who promptly falls in love with 'Cesario'. Alongside this plot, Olivia's uncle and his friends add comedy to the play by playing tricks on Olivia's pompous steward, Malvolio. Eventually – surprise, surprise – Viola's true identity is revealed, Viola and Sebastian find each other, and the main characters are happily married, Viola to Orsino and Olivia to Sebastian.

KEY QUOTATIONS

❋ Orsino:

> *If music be the food of love, play on,*
> *Give me excess of it that surfeiting,*
> *The appetite may sicken, and so die.*

❋ The trick letter to Malvolio, which he reads:

> *Some are born great, some achieve greatness, and some have*
> *greatness thrust upon them*

7 The Tragedies and Dark Comedies

ALL'S WELL THAT ENDS WELL

This is a dark comedy, and a very serious play. Nevertheless, it is a tale about love, and in that sense a romantic comedy. Like most of Shakespeare's dark comedies, *All's Well That Ends Well* was written in the second half of his career; and this is the earliest of them. It is a play designed to stimulate thought and even to shock; it treats sexual love in a way which Shakespeare's audiences would have found quite unsettling.

KEY CHARACTERS

Bertram Count of Rossillion.

The Countess His mother, kindly disposed towards Helena.

Helena A young girl brought up by the Countess.

King of France Helena saves his life with one of her father's medicines.

Widow A widow living in Florence who befriends Helena.

Diana The widow's daughter, with whom Bertram is in love.

The story

Helena loves Bertram, but he has no time for her. In any case, she is beneath him, being only the daughter of a physician. However, when she saves the King's life, he rewards her by allowing her to choose a husband from any of the noblemen at his court. She chooses Bertram. He is extremely annoyed and, straight after the wedding, sends her home to his mother. He swears he will never treat her as a wife unless, among other things, she becomes pregnant by him. Since he also insists that he will never consummate the marriage, this looks a little tricky to accomplish.

However, Helena manages it by changing places with a young woman with whom Bertram is in love. After many turns of the plot, her deceit is eventually revealed, and Bertram realizes that he loves Helena after all.

CYMBELINE

This is another of the dark comedies although it is not generally regarded as one of Shakespeare's best. In his *Notes on Shakespeare* Dr Jonson (1709–1784) comments on its 'unresisting imbecility' which is perhaps a little harsh, but it certainly verges on the corny in places. However, some of the great speeches are beautifully written, and are typical of Shakespeare's style: *Cymbeline* was one of his last plays, probably written in about 1609.

The story

Imogen, daughter of King Cymbeline, secretly marries Posthumus, her father's adopted son, to escape marriage to her step-brother Cloten, a boorish and unpleasant man. But Cymbeline is furious, and banishes Posthumus, who goes off to Rome. There he befriends Iachimo, who bets him that he can win Imogen from him – no woman can be that faithful. Iachimo travels to England and fails to win Imogen, but tricks her into providing 'proof' that he has, which devastates Posthumus.

Imogen ends up lost in the forest, dressed as a boy, while trying to follow Posthumus to Rome. There she meets up with her twin brothers, who had been stolen as babies and given up for dead. Cloten dresses as Posthumus to pursue her and the confusion deepens. Cloten is killed, and everyone else finally meets up, the king rediscovers his long lost sons, and everyone lives happily ever after.

HAMLET

This is arguably Shakespeare's best-known play. But why? Well, it's as good a study as you'll find anywhere of a mind in torment. As well as having an absorbing plot (not Shakespeare's own, of course), *Hamlet* has some beautiful writing and a central character whose situation – and the way he handles it – are gripping and utterly convincing. Hamlet's famous soliloquies give us an insight in to the deepest workings of his mind as he battles with his conscience over whether to kill his uncle as revenge for his poisoning Hamlet's father.

Hamlet is also a lesson in madness. Hamlet himself tries to escape the same fate as his father by pretending to be mad, so that no one will see him as a threat. His pretence is so good that we almost wonder if he really has gone mad. However, just as we reach this point, Ophelia goes truly mad, making us realize what real madness is, and putting Hamlet's complex and angst-ridden – but ultimately sane – behaviour back in context.

Some people have suggested that the character of Hamlet, if not his situation, was semi-autobiographical. There is no evidence to support this, but Shakespeare does seem to have put more effort into writing *Hamlet* than any other play. It was probably revised over a long period, and it is significantly the longest of all the plays. It is an important play in the history of English literature because Hamlet represents the first example, and perhaps still the greatest, of a modern man complete with anxieties, uncertainties and complexities of thought: a thoroughly fascinating character with whom the audience cannot fail to sympathise.

KEY CHARACTERS

Hamlet Son of the murdered King of Denmark, he swears revenge on his uncle, who killed Hamlet's father and then married his mother.

Claudius The new King, now married to his brother's wife. He will murder Hamlet if necessary to keep his throne, and Hamlet knows it.

Gertrude She loves Hamlet, with whom there are hints of an Oedipus-like affection. But she is fickle and she upsets Hamlet deeply by remarrying so soon after the King's death.

Polonius An old man, advisor to the King, who is good but irritates everyone by talking too much. Hamlet kills him by mistake: he is eavesdropping behind a curtain and Hamlet thinks he is Claudius.

Ophelia Polonius' daughter who is deeply in love with Hamlet, who has appeared to reciprocate her love in the past. But he rejects her in his single-minded search for revenge, and she goes mad and drowns.

The story

The ghost of Hamlet's father appears to him and tells him that he was poisoned by Claudius; he commands Hamlet to take revenge. But Claudius is now married to Hamlet's mother. Hamlet is racked with guilt and conscience, and the play is about how Hamlet brings himself to kill his uncle. In the final scene, Claudius and Gertrude are both killed, along with Laertes (Ophelia's brother), and Hamlet himself.

KEY QUOTATIONS

* Hamlet contemplating suicide:
  To be, or not to be: that is the question...

* Hamlet longing for death:
  O! That this too too solid flesh would melt,
  Thaw and resolve itself into a dew...

* Polonius giving advice to his son:
  Neither a borrower, nor a lender be...

* Ophelia gone mad:
  There's rosemary, that's for remembrance; pray, love,
  remember

* Hamlet on finding the skull of the old jester in the graveyard:
  Alas! Poor Yorick. I knew him, Horatio; a fellow of infinite
  jest...

* Horatio's farewell to Hamlet as he dies:
  ... Good night, sweet prince,
  And flights of angels sing thee to thy rest!

* Hamlet's final words:
  ... The rest is silence.

KING LEAR

This is another of Shakespeare's great tragedies, and another contender for the top spot of 'Shakespeare's best ever play'. If you're not used to reading Shakespeare, *King Lear* can be quite hard to get to grips with because it contains so much complex thought. This is largely because Shakespeare was more concerned, in this play, with examining behaviour than with telling a story. The lines often seem to fall over each other, and complex imagery and ideas are packed in to them. Often the standard iambic pentameter rhythm is drowned in the onslaught.

The play is a study of descent into madness bound up in how human experience affects character, and, in Lear's case, drives him mad. Everything in the play – ideas, assumptions, attitudes, even identities – seem to be constantly shifting and developing, so that it is hard for the audience to find anything to grasp on to, just as it is impossible for Lear himself.

KEY CHARACTERS

King Lear The old King, who divides his country between two of his daughters. He casts out his third and – until then – favourite daughter, because she will not say that she loves him more than anyone else.

Cordelia Lear's daughter, punished for being honest and saying that she will love her husband as much as she loves her father.

Goneril and **Regan** Lear's two wicked daughters, who claim to love him and then abandon him.

Gloucester A nobleman who is falsely persuaded that his eldest son is plotting against him. He is eventually blinded by Regan and her husband.

Edgar Gloucester's elder son, who disguises himself as a madman (Poor Tom) and runs away when his father believes he is disloyal.

Edmund Gloucester's bastard younger son, who persuades him to mistrust Edgar. Edmund is an out-and-out baddie, but at the very end of the play he tries to prevent Lear and Cordelia being executed.

Kent Lear's loyal follower, who sticks by him and stays in communication with Cordelia after her banishment.

The Fool The only one allowed to criticize Lear, the Fool is perhaps the wisest character of all.

The story

Lear banishes Cordelia for her refusal to say she loves him above all else, and divides his kingdom between his other two daughters. They turn against him and he realizes too late his mistake in favouring them over the honest Cordelia. He gradually goes mad, wracked with torment at what he has done to Cordelia. Cordelia who has married the King of France, returns with an army to save him, but they are captured by Goneril and Regan. Cordelia and Lear are reunited in prison, but the order comes to execute them. The death-warrant is stopped by Edmund, but too late – Cordelia has already been hanged, and Lear dies of grief over her body.

KEY QUOTATIONS

✳ Lear to Cordelia when they are captured:
> *Come, let's away to prison;*
> *We two alone will sing like birds i'the cage:*
> *When thou dost ask me blessing. I'll kneel down,*
> *And ask of thee forgiveness…*

✳ Lear on Cordelia's death:
> *… No, no, no life!*
> *Why should a dog, a horse, a rat have life,*
> *And thou no breath at all? Thou'it come no more;*
> *Never, never, never, never, never*

✳ Edgar at the close of the play:
> *The weight of this sad time we must obey;*
> *Speak what we feel, not what we ought to say.*

MACBETH

This play is all about a central character brought down by his own excessive ambition. At the start of the play, Macbeth is loyal to the King, Duncan, and has a reputation as a good man and a soldier. But his wife, Lady Macbeth, tells him he is loyal only because he is afraid of the consequences of disloyalty. As she says, he 'would not play false, And yet wouldst wrongly win'. When the witches tempt him to the throne with their prophecy that he shall 'be king hereafter', he is still indecisive about whether to kill Duncan. Eventually, persuaded by his powerful wife, he resolves to do it.

As Macbeth, who was initially weak in his resolve, progresses, he becomes stronger and more single-minded in his determination to fulfill his ambition. He orders the brutal murder of Macduff's wife and children, and shows little grief even when his own wife dies. By contrast Lady Macbeth begins the play strong and ruthless, but the murders affect her in the opposite way from her husband and she becomes mad, eventually killing herself.

KEY CHARACTERS

Macbeth Thane of Glamis, later King of Scotland.

Lady Macbeth His wife.

Duncan King of Scotland, murdered by Macbeth.

Malcolm Duncan's eldest son and rightful heir.

Banquo A friend of Macbeth's at the start of the play, but later murdered by him.

Macduff Another Thane who suspects Macbeth and helps Malcolm to defeat him and regain the crown.

The story

On a heath in Scotland, Macbeth and Banquo meet three witches, who predict that Macbeth will become Thane of Cawdor and subsequently King of Scotland. Shortly after this, he is unexpectedly made Thane of Cawdor, and he begins to think about the witches' prophecy. Lady Macbeth learns of the witches prediction and persuades Macbeth to kill Duncan and then Banquo. Malcolm, Duncan's eldest son, has fled Scotland and joined with Macduff, and they plan to bring an army against Macbeth. Meanwhile, Lady Macbeth has taken to sleepwalking, trying to wash the blood of Duncan from her hands.

Eventually Macbeth is isolated and surrounded by Malcolm's troops. He is brought the news that his wife has killed herself. Macduff meets Macbeth on the battlefield and kills him, and Malcolm is crowned King.

KEY QUOTATIONS

* Lady Macbeth speaking about her husband's nature:
    It is too full o' the milk of human kindness
    To catch the nearest way: thou wouldst be great,
    Art not without ambition, but without
    The illness should attend it…

* Lady Macbeth planning to kill Duncan:
    … Come you spirits
    That tend on mortal thoughts! Unsex me here
    And fill me from the crown to the toe top full
    Of direst cruelty; make thick my blood,
    Stop up the access and passage to remorse…

* Macbeth's vision:
    Is this a dagger that I see before me,
    The handle towards my hand? Come, let me clutch thee.
    I have thee not, and yet I see thee still.

* Macbeth:
    Methought I heard a voice cry 'Sleep no more!
    Macbeth doth murder sleep' – the innocent sleep,
    Sleep that knits up the ravelled sleeve of care…

* Lady Macbeth sleepwalking:
    Out, damned spot! Out, I say!… who would have thought the old man to have had so much blood in him?

MEASURE FOR MEASURE

Critics and scholars have always found it hard to agree on this play. It is certainly one of Shakespeare's best plays, but it is open to many different interpretations. It is modern in its treatment of lust, and of men's response to it. But what about the character of Angelo, whose dishonest lust (as opposed to Claudio's more honest version) is at the core of the play?

Angelo can be seen either as a wicked villain, or as an intrinsically good man who is wracked with guilt over his weakness for Isabella. Isabella, likewise, can appear as anything from a worldly young woman to a cold, chaste saint. The difficulty for critics with this play is that it is so complex, and even contradictory, that it is surprisingly hard to interpret.

KEY CHARACTERS

The Duke Vincentio, a wise but lenient ruler.

Angelo Deputy to the Duke.

Claudio A young gentleman, who is living with **Juliet** but not married to her.

Isabella Claudio's sister.

Mariana Betrothed to Angelo.

The story

The Duke of Vienna leaves his dukedom in the hands of Angelo, a saintly man. Angelo, more strict than the Duke, enforces an ancient and almost forgotten law which says that any man living with a woman out of wedlock should be executed. He condemns a young man, Claudio, to death. Claudio's sister, Isabella, who has just entered a convent, pleads with Angelo to pardon her brother. Angelo is smitten by Isabella, and tells her that if she will sleep with him, he will pardon Claudio. Isabella is horrified, but doesn't think anyone will believe her if she accuses Angelo publicly. Luckily, however, the Duke has been in Vienna all along, posing as a friar, and overhears Isabella telling Claudio what Angelo has said. He ensures that everything is resolved, and Claudio is pardoned.

OTHELLO

Another of Shakespeare's four 'great tragedies', *Othello* is about jealousy. It contains some of the finest language in any of Shakespeare's plays, as well as being a beautifully constructed drama.

In this play, Shakespeare uses the two standard formats of prose and blank verse to deliberate effect. Iago, whose own jealousy of Cassio prompts him to trick Othello into being jealous, speaks mostly in prose. However, when he is on his own, and in an emotional state, Iago switches into blank verse – the natural medium of emotion in all the plays. Othello, by contrast, naturally speaks in blank verse, but falls into prose when he is overcome with emotion.

Just as *King Lear* shows us a man descending into madness, and *Macbeth* shows us a man descending into evil, so *Othello* shows a descent too, this time into jealousy. Othello's progress from denial, through doubt, to eventual belief in Desdemona's unfaithfulness is painful to watch.

The most interesting character of all, even more than Othello, is Iago. Othello promotes Cassio instead of Iago, which makes Iago so angry that he resolves to have revenge on them both. However, he is the cleverest of villains, deceiving even his own wife, and is so universally thought to be good and reliable that he is regularly referred to as 'honest Iago'.

KEY CHARACTERS

Othello The Moor, a dignified, sensible and well-loved military leader.

Desdemona Othello's new wife.

Iago A clever man, who appears honest and good but plots to bring down all his enemies.

Cassio Othello's lieutenant, a charming and honest courtier.

The story
When Othello promotes Cassio instead of Iago to the position of lieutenant, Iago swears to himself that he will have his revenge. He convinces everyone that he is honest and a true friend, but in fact he schemes and plots to persuade Othello that his beautiful young wife, Desdemona, is unfaithful to him. At first Othello refuses to believe him, but Iago is very

convincing. He gradually succeeds in making Othello believe that Desdemona is seeing Cassio behind his back. In his fury, Othello kills the innocent Desdemona. When he learns, moments later, that he was tricked by Iago, he is so grief-stricken that he kills himself.

KEY QUOTATIONS

* Iago to Othello:
    > *O, beware, my lord, of jealousy!*
    > *It is the green-eyed monster, which doth mock*
    > *The meat it feeds on.*

* Othello's jealousy:
    > *… I had rather be a toad,*
    > *And live upon the vapour of a dungeon,*
    > *Than keep a corner in the thing I love*
    > *For others' uses.*

* Iago on Othello's jealousy:
    > *… Not poppy, nor mandragora,*
    > *Nor all the drowsy syrups of the world,*
    > *Shall ever medicine thee to that sweet sleep*
    > *Which thou owed'st yesterday.*

* Othello, carrying a light, to Desdemona as she sleeps just before he kills her:
    > *Put out the light, and then put out the light…*

* Othello on how he would like to be remembered:
    > *When you shall these unlucky deeds relate…*
    > *Of one that loved not wisely, but too well…*

* Othello's dying words:
    > *I kissed thee, ere I killed thee: no way but this,*
    > *Killing myself, to die upon a kiss.*

ROMEO AND JULIET

This is the most often performed of all Shakespeare's plays. It is the best of his early plays (he wrote it around 1594), although it lacks the greatness of some of his later plays. It is, thanks to Shakespeare, one of the best-known tragic love stories in the world.

The prologue calls the lovers 'star-crossed', meaning that their fate was in the stars all along, and there is frequent reference to the characters' destinies being in the stars. In many ways, this play is a catalogue of bad luck, although Romeo's impetuousness means that he seems to court bad luck. At one point the friar prophetically says to him: 'Wisely and slow. They stumble that run fast.'

Romeo and Juliet is a play about hate as much as a play about love. Shakespeare repeatedly impresses on us that the lovers would not have died had not their two families hated each other so unnecessarily. It is also about many different kinds of love: Romeo and Juliet's young love; Romeo's infatuation with his earlier love, Rosaline, whom he forgets as soon as he sees Juliet; the dutiful love Capulet expects from his daughter and the courtly love of Paris for Juliet.

KEY CHARACTERS

Romeo A young man, son of Lord Montague.

Juliet Only fourteen years old, the daughter of Lord and Lady Capulet.

Tybalt Juliet's cousin, a hot-tempered young man who loves fighting.

Mercutio A friend of Romeo, a likeable, witty young man, who is killed in a brawl by Tybalt.

The nurse Juliet's nurse, her ally and in on the secret about Romeo.

The story

Romeo and Juliet belong to rival families in Verona. They meet and fall in love and, knowing their families would never countenance their marriage, they marry in secret. Romeo then kills Tybalt and is banished. Juliet's father tries to marry her off, not knowing she is already married to Romeo.

To escape from committing bigamy – or admitting her marriage to Romeo – Juliet takes a potion which makes her appear to be dead. She is laid in the family vault where Romeo is supposed to meet her when she wakes up and when they plan to they will run away together. However, messages get lost and Romeo thinks she is really dead, so he kills himself. Moments later, she awakes and, finding her husband dead beside her, she too kills herself.

KEY QUOTATIONS

* Romeo seeing Juliet on the balcony:
    But soft! What light through yonder window breaks?
    It is the east, and Juliet is the sun!

* Juliet on Romeo's name (being a Montague):
    O Romeo, Romeo! Wherefore art thou Romeo?
    … What's in a name? That which we call a rose
    By any other name would smell as sweet…

* Juliet's farewell to Romeo:
    Good-night, good-night! Parting is such sweet sorrow
    That I shall say good-night till it be morrow.

* Romeo to Juliet, believing her to be dead:
    … O my love, my wife!
    Death, that hath sucked the honey of thy breath,
    Hath had no power yet upon thy beauty.
    Thou art not conquered. Beauty's ensign yet
    Is crimson in thy lips and in thy cheeks,
    And death's pale flag is not advancèd there.

* Romeo's dying words:
    … Eyes, look your last!
    Arms, take your last embrace! And lips, O you
    The doors of breath, seal with a righteous kiss
    A dateless bargain to engrossing death!
    … Here's to my love! O true Apothecary!
    Thy drugs are quick. Thus with a kiss I die.

THE TWO NOBLE KINSMEN

This play, probably Shakespeare's last, was long excluded from the Shakespeare canon, and from versions of the *Complete Works*. The original version, printed in 1634, states clearly that it was written by John Fletcher (a prominent actor and a friend of Shakespeare) and William Shakespeare. However, it was not included in any collection of his plays until 1841, and even then was not widely accepted as being his. However, in the last fifty or sixty years scholars have become increasingly certain that Shakespeare wrote a substantial part of the play. Some sections are written in such mature Shakespearean style that most experts don't believe any other writer of the time was capable of producing them.

The story

The plot of the play was a popular story at the time, told by Boccaccio and Chaucer among others. Palamon and Arcite are two handsome cousins, both knights, who are imprisoned after battle. They see a beautiful girl from their prison window and both fall in love with her. She turns out to be Emilia, sister-in-law of Theseus, Duke of Athens. This conflict is central to the play; eventually the two men fight a duel after which the loser shall be beheaded. Arcite wins but, just before Palamon is executed, Arcite falls from his horse and dies, leaving Palamon to marry Emilia.

THE WINTER'S TALE

In Shakespeare's day, the expression 'a winter's tale' meant an improbable and fantastic tale, often a ghost story. This play was very probably written immediately before *The Tempest* and, while it is not such a masterpiece, there are echoes of *The Tempest* here. In both plays, it is somehow the most fantastical events with which we can identify most closely – they seem more real than everyday events. The implausibility of the plot helps, rather than hinders, our belief in it. The title also refers, however, to the long winter which Leontes creates around himself by managing to lose his wife and both his children through his own fault.

The story

Leontes and his wife, Hermione, are happy until his old friend Polixenes comes to visit. Leontes gets it into his head that his friend and his wife are having an affair, and he convinces himself it is true. Polixenes finds this out and flees back to his own country, Bohemia. Leontes imprisons Hermione, who is pregnant, and refuses her permission to see their young son. When the baby is born, Leontes refuses to acknowledge his daughter and orders the baby to be taken across the sea and abandoned somewhere. His son dies grieving for his mother, and Hermione too dies of grief. Leontes realizes his mistake too late, and goes into mourning.

So Perdita, Leontes' baby daughter, grows up not knowing who she is, but believing herself a humble shepherdess. It so happens that Polixenes son, Florizel, meets her and falls in love with her. They elope (since his father won't let him marry her), and they end up back at Leontes' court. Perdita's identity is discovered, and Paulina, Hermione's old lady-in-waiting, invites everyone to see a statue of Hermione she has commissioned. As they admire the statue it appears to come to life; in fact it is Hermione, who has been alive all the time, waiting in secret for her daughter to be found. Everyone forgives Leontes, and Perdita and Florizel are married.

The Histories

8

KING JOHN

It is worth remembering that King John lived about four hundred years before Shakespeare, so Shakespeare was writing about events from long ago. To put this in perspective, we are now living about four hundred years after Shakespeare. King John argued with the Pope, and was therefore often seen in sixteenth-century England as an early Protestant. Shakespeare wrote this play at a time when England was under threat of war from Spain and France, even after the successful defeat of the Armada, and it would have struck a patriotic chord with his contemporary audiences. The closing speech, given by the Bastard, is almost jingoistic in tone.

The Bastard (brother of King John) is an interesting character, almost unheard of historically, yet Shakespeare persuades us that he is the most likely person to succeed to the throne. We forget, watching the play, that we know historically that John was succeeded by Henry III (you did know that, didn't you? Shakespeare's audience would have done!).

The story

The play deals with several of the events of King John's reign, including the death of his nephew, Arthur, an innocent child, who threatens his throne. It also deals with the war with France, King John's conflict with the Pope, and ends with his death by poisoning at Swinstead Abbey.

KEY QUOTATION

* The Bastard's closing lines:
    This England never did, nor never shall,
    Lie at the proud foot of a conqueror
    But when it first did help to wound itself…

RICHARD II

The most striking thing about this play is the contrasting characters and fortunes of Richard and Bolingbroke. King Richard begins by banishing

Bolingbroke, and ends disposessed by him. We certainly sympathize with Richard, but his behaviour can be rash, and he is not a great king. Bolingbroke, by contrast, has no right to the throne, but he is a strong character and promises to be a better king than Richard. As usual, Shakespeare does not give us a simple moral right and wrong situation.

This play tells the story of the cause of the wars of the roses. Bolingbroke is the son of John of Gaunt, Duke of Lancaster. Richard is supported by the Duke of York and his son. Lancaster and York are both uncles of Richard's – both brothers of his father the late king Edward III.

The story

At the start of the play, Richard exiles his cousin, Henry Bolingbroke for five years. When Henry's father, John of Gaunt, dies, Richard confiscates his property. Bolingbroke then invades England while Richard is abroad. On his return he is humiliated by Bolingbroke and is forced to abdicate. Bolingbroke – now Henry IV – imprisons him and finally has him murdered.

KEY QUOTATIONS

✳ John of Gaunt on England:

> *This royal throne of kings, this scepter'd isle,*
> *This earth of majesty, this seat of Mars,*
> *This other Eden, demi-paradise,*
> *This fortress built by Nature for herself*
> *Against infection and the hand of war,*
> *This happy breed of men, this little world…*

✳ King Richard:

> *Not all the water in the rough rude sea*
> *Can wash the balm from an anointed king…*

✳ King Richard:

> *For God's sake, let us sit upon the ground*
> *And tell sad stories of the death of kings…*

HENRY IV PART 1

Although Shakespeare did not write his history plays in chronological order, the subject matter of this play follows on from *Richard II*. Bolingbroke is now established as Henry IV, but he is troubled by his wayward son, Hal, who spends more time cavorting with Falstaff than behaving like a future king.

The play focuses on the rebellion led by Henry Percy, Earl of Northumberland, and his son, Harry Hotspur (yes, all four of the leading characters are called Henry). The two sons, Prince Hal and Hotspur are set up as enemies, and yet we hardly know whose side to take. The trouble is they are both heroic, characters. This is not a play about goodies and baddies; it is a true story of a conflict with right and wrong on both sides. These young men are not tainted with the corruption, greed or guilt of their fathers, and both deserve to succeed.

The play is also about the conversion of Prince Hal, which was legendary in Shakespeare's time. He spends much time in the company of Falstaff

– one of Shakespeare's most popular characters then and now – playing the fool, drinking and behaving in a way that disappoints his father deeply. And yet when things get serious, he manages to act like a true Prince of Wales, and one who will plausibly later become the heroic Henry V.

KEY CHARACTERS

King Henry IV Formerly Henry Bolingbroke, who deposed Richard II.

Prince Hal The wayward Prince of Wales.

Henry Percy Earl of Northumberland.

Harry Hotspur Hot-headed son of Henry Percy.

Sir John Falstaff Prince Hal's dissolute companion, and the source of most of the humour in the play.

The story

The Percys rebel against King Henry and bring an army against him. His son, Prince Hal, spends most of his time drinking and carousing with Falstaff and shows little interest in matters of state. However, when the time comes, he joins the battle against Percy and Hotspur, and kills Hotspur himself (although Falstaff entertainingly claims that it was he who killed Hotspur).

KEY QUOTATIONS

❋ Prince Hal to Hotspur:
> *Two stars keep not their motion in one sphere.*

❋ Prince Hal over Hotspur's body:
> *Fare thee well, great heart!*
> *Ill-weav'd ambition, how much art thou shrunk!*
> *When that this body did contain a spirit,*
> *A kingdom for it was to small a bound;*
> *But now two paces of the vilest earth*
> *Is room enough…*

HENRY IV PART II

Like all of Shakespeare's history plays, this one stands alone. It is not the second half of the previous play – in fact, we don't even know whether Shakespeare intended to write this play at all when he first wrote the earlier part of Henry IV. Certainly this play is very different from *Henry IV Part I*. Its mood is more sombre, although it still contains much comedy from Falstaff and his companions.

Falstaff is once again a brilliant comic character, large and rumbustious, and always looking for tricks to play and jokes to make. But he believes – or seems to believe – that when Hal becomes king he will make Falstaff one of his chief advisers. It is obvious to us, and to Hal, that this would be impossible. In *Henry IV Part II*, Shakespeare is preparing Prince Hal to become a noble king – even going so far as to stop calling him Hal and call him Prince Henry instead. The play has a sombre note, with Prince Henry aware that he will soon have to take on the duty of kingship. When his father dies, and he accedes the throne, it is no real surprise to anyone but Falstaff that the new King rejects him. And yet Falstaff is such an appealing and real character that, even though we see it is inevitable, his rejection is deeply painful to watch.

The story

King Henry IV has yet another rebellion to deal with, this time from Archbishop Scroop, Mowbray and Hastings. Falstaff is recruited to the army to help put down the rebellion, and falls in with two justices, Shallow and Silence. After the rebellion is successfully quashed, King Henry dies and Prince Henry becomes King (Henry V). Falstaff expects

---

KEY QUOTATION

✳ King Henry IV:
> *Uneasy lies the head that wears a crown.*

✳ *King Henry V rejects Falstaff:*
> *I know thee not, old man: fall to thy prayers;*
> *How ill white hairs become a fool and jester!*

to be given high office, but the new King disowns him and has him thrown into prison.

HENRY V

Henry V is Shakespeare's great hero king. This is the last of all the histories, written in 1599. It can be dated more accurately than almost any other play because it makes direct reference to the expedition of the Earl of Essex to put down rebellion in Ireland. The chorus says:

> *Were now the General of our gracious Empress –*
> *As in good time he may – from Ireland coming,*
> *Bringing rebellion broachèd on his sword…*

Essex left England in March 1599 and returned – unsuccessful – in September the same year. So the play was clearly written between these dates, at a time when everyone was feeling patriotic and expecting great things. This is reflected in the mood of the play.

Shakespeare's audiences needed a patriotic fillip in any case, since war with Spain and France was always threatening until the death of Queen Elizabeth in 1603. *Henry V* does the job so well that it has often been performed since in times of national danger. A film of *Henry V*, starring Laurence Olivier, was made during World War II in order to give the public an uplifting sense of patriotism. In the context of the cycle of Shakespeare's history plays, and of historical fact, Henry V's reign really was a shining light between the dark and trouble-torn reigns around it.

The play has been criticized by scholars for being historically inaccurate, for glossing over some of Henry's faults, and for being sentimentally patriotic in places. However, to the ordinary audience rather than the scholar, this play has huge energy, great honesty and a wonderfully charismatic hero as its central character. You might nitpick with it; but, you cannot help but love watching such a rollicking drama.

The story

Henry sets out with an army for France. He captures Harfleur and wins a magnificent victory against the odds at Agincourt. He then woos

Katharine, Princess of France, and marries her, uniting the two countries. Several of Falstaff's old companions appear having been called up as soldiers, and during the play the death of Falstaff (who never actually appears) is announced to them.

KEY QUOTATIONS

✳ Chorus at the start of the play:
> *O! for a Muse of fire, that would ascend*
> *The brightest heaven of invention…*

✳ Chorus on the preparations for war:
> *Now all the youth of England are on fire,*
> *And silken dalliance in the wardrobe lies…*

✳ Henry urging his troops to battle at Harfleur:
> *Once more unto the breach, dear friends, once more;*
> *Or close the wall up with our English dead!*
> *In peace there's nothing so becomes a man*
> *As modest stillness and humility:*
> *But when the blast of war blows in our ears,*
> *Then imitate the action of the tiger…*
> *I see you stand like greyhounds in the slips,*
> *Straining upon the start. The game's afoot:*
> *Follow your spirit; and, upon this charge*
> *Cry 'God for Harry! England and Saint George!'*

HENRY VI PART 1

The three parts of *Henry VI* are thought to be Shakespeare's three earliest plays (although *Part I* may well have come just after the other two parts). Each is a complete play in its own right, and each deals with a different aspect of Henry's reign. *Part I* deals with the war with France, against the army led by Joan of Arc.

Following the popular view at the time Shakespeare wrote the play, Joan of Arc is represented as a 'minister of hell'. When Shakespeare was writing the play, England had troops in France supporting the French claimant to the throne, and he would have had this very much in mind. The play may seem like ancient history now, but it would have had an immediate relevance then, even though it referred to events over a hundred and fifty years previously.

It is generally accepted that Shakepeare did not write these three plays alone. Either he co-wrote them, or he heavily revised someone else's work. However, we do not know who else worked on them, although all sorts of possible co-authors have been suggested, including Christopher Marlowe.

The story

Henry VI Part I is essentially about the disintegration of England's power in Europe. It opens with the funeral of Henry V, and goes on to deal with France's gradual expulsion of England from continental soil, and in particular with the inspirational French leader, Joan of Arc, through her successful career and then her fall. Meanwhile, in England, Henry is faced with quarrelling amongst his nobles, and the beginning of the conflict between the houses of York and Lancaster.

HENRY VI PART II

This play is a progression from order to chaos. At the start of the play Henry is in control, albeit weakly, of his own country. But everyone is against him – his wife, his noblemen, the public – and all abandon him – the rule of law and justice falls down – Suffolk and his cronies kill Gloucester precisely because they know that the law would not condemn him, so there's no point having him tried. As the play goes on, less and less value is attached to goodness and Christian virtue, and civil war is inevitable by the end.

Henry VI and Gloucester represent the forces of good and order in the play, and it is the other characters' reactions to these qualities that bring the structure of the country down. It is obvious that this is one of Shakespeare's earliest plays – probably the first – and this can be seen in the language of the play and in its handling of the subject. In terms of language, Shakespeare adheres firmly to iambic pentameter with plenty of rhyming couplets, and none of the variety and freedom of style of his later plays. Where the content is concerned, many of the characters resemble characters out of miracle plays, which had been the staple dramatic diet only a few decades before (see Chapter 2). Both Gloucester and the pious Henry have a saint-like quality, while the Queen and Suffolk, in particular, have few redeeming qualities.

The story

The play starts with King Henry's marriage to Margaret of Anjou, a spirited woman for whom the pious Henry is no match, and who is carrying on an affair with Suffolk. The Queen, Suffolk and others conspire against Gloucester, the King's uncle and Protector of England, and kill him. Suffolk is eventually killed too. The other key event in the play is the uprising led by Jack Cade. Although Cade is killed in the end, Henry's England is now irreparably broken.

HENRY VI PART III

This play, one of Shakespeare's earliest, cannot frankly be considered one of his better works. It lacks any real sense of development or climax; the action pulls back and forth between the warring parties in a series of episodes, not unlike the Wars of the Roses themselves, as King Henry says:

> *Now sways it this way like a mighty sea*
> *Forced by the tide to combat with the wind;*
> *Now sways it that way, like the self-same sea*
> *Forced to retire by fury of the wind.*

The story

Henry VI surrenders his succession to the crown to the Duke of York after the Battle of Saint Albans. However, Queen Margaret takes exception to her son being disinherited, and revolts against her husband. There are various battles back and forth – the Wars of the Roses – during which the Duke of York is killed, but his son, Edward, takes over the title. The play ends with the Battle of Tewkesbury, where Edward, Prince of Wales, is killed and Queen Margaret taken prisoner. The young Duke of York is proclaimed King Edward IV. Finally, King Henry is murdered in the Tower of London by the unscrupulous Richard, Duke of Gloucester (who later becomes Richard III).

KEY QUOTATION

❋ Henry musing on the trials of kingship:

> *O God! Methinks it were a happy life,*
> *To be no better than a homely swain;*
> *To sit upon a hill, as I do now,*
> *To carve out dials, quaintly, point by point,*
> *Thereby to see the minutes how they run*
> *How many make the hour full complete;*
> *How many hours bring about the day;*
> *How many days will finish up the year;*
> *How many years a mortal man may live.*

RICHARD III

This play, one of Shakespeare's most popular ever since it was first written, owes its success to the character of Richard. He is one of the great stage villains, whose character Shakespeare drew, with only a little artistic licence, from the chronicles of Hall and Holinshed (see Chapter 5). They were biased, of course, since Richard was finally defeated by Queen Elizabeth's grandfather – to make his dubious claim to the throne appear justified they needed to paint Richard as very black.

Although the portrait of Richard may be unfair on the historical man himself, it certainly makes for great theatre. He is malicious, crafty, envious, clever and witty, and, although we hate him, we thoroughly enjoy doing so. We are let in on his intentions from the start, and are privy to his secret thoughts and plans. We watch as he carefully edges closer and closer to the throne only to lose it almost as soon as he has won it.

KEY CHARACTERS

King Edward IV

Edward, Prince of Wales (later King Edward V) and **Richard, Duke of York** The young princes, known as the 'princes in the Tower'.

George, Duke of Clarence Brother of the King.

Richard, Duke of Gloucester Younger brother of the King, later Richard III.

Lady Anne Widow of the previous Edward, Prince of Wales, the son of Henry VI, who marries Richard.

The story

Richard, Duke of Gloucester, is ambitious for his brother's crown. He woos Lady Anne over the body of her dead father-in-law (killed by Richard) and persuades Anne to marry him. She is the daughter of Warwick (known as Warwick the Kingmaker), and a useful political gain. Richard's elder brother, Clarence, is ahead of him in line to the throne, so he has him killed. When Edward IV dies, and is succeeded by his young son, Edward V, Richard imprisons the young king and his brother in the Tower and later murders them.

Richard is now King, but the forces of Henry Tudor are gathering. Richard meets them on the battlefield at Bosworth and is defeated and killed; Henry Tudor is crowned Henry VII.

KEY QUOTATIONS

✳ Richard's opening lines:

> *Now is the winter of our discontent*
> *Made glorious summer by this son of York*

✳ Richard on the battlefield:

> *A horse! A horse! My kingdom for a horse!*

HENRY VIII

This is almost the last of Shakespeare's plays, perhaps even the very last, and it is quite likely that not all of it was written by him. It deals with two main subjects: Henry's divorce from Catherine of Aragon, and the fall of Cardinal Wolsey. Shakespeare is rigorously true to his sources – chiefly Holinshed as usual – in his telling of events. *Henry VIII* is not an outstanding play, but Shakespeare has taken a true story and retold it honestly, in a way that makes for interesting and powerful drama.

The story

Henry wants the Pope to annul his marriage to Catherine of Aragon, ostensibly because he claims it isn't legal, but actually so that he can marry his lover, Anne Boleyn. Catherine is deeply upset and, when the Pope supports her, Henry overrules him and declares that he is the supreme head of the Church of England.

Meanwhile the avaricious Cardinal Wolsey is so compromised by this situation that he is left friendless and stripped of all his honours and wealth. Henry marries Anne Boleyn, Thomas Cranmer becomes arch-bishop and triumphs over his enemies, and Anne gives birth to a daughter. The christening of the baby princess, who will grow up to become Queen Elizabeth II, is the closing scene of the play.

The Classical Plays

9

ANTONY AND CLEOPATRA

Sixty years after Shakespeare's death John Dryden (1631–1700) wrote an adaptation of it called *All For Love* (1677) which was much more popular at the time, and Shakespeare's play was hardly performed for the next two hundred years.

Despite its subject matter, this is not a grand or spectacular play. It consists of short scenes between small numbers of characters, giving it a feeling of intimacy. It is the only one of the Roman plays without any crowd scenes (the other Roman plays being *Julius Caesar* and *Coriolanus*).

The story of Antony and Cleopatra was already a stock theme for dramatists by the time Shakespeare wrote his version. It was always presented in the classical style, adhering to the three unities of Greek tragedy: time, place and action. In other words, the plays invariably took place in real time, in a single setting, and told a single uncomplicated plot. So it was always necessary to tell the last two hours or so of the hero and heroine's life.

Shakespeare was the first writer to attempt to tell the story of Antony and Cleopatra in a narrative style, giving a sense of the passage of time. Like the other playwrights before him, Shakespeare used as his source Plutarch's *Parallel Lives*, and he adhered closely to Plutarch's theme. Plutarch was interested in establishing what kind of a man Mark Antony was, and in relating anecdotes and small events to illuminate his subject's life. Shakespeare followed this style himself in writing what was, at the time, a revolutionary new telling of an old story.

KEY CHARACTERS

Mark Antony One of the three triumvirs, who rule Rome together.

Cleopatra Queen of Egypt.

Octavius Caesar Another of the triumvirs.

Octavia Caesar's sister, who marries Mark Antony.

Enobarbus A friend of Antony's.

The story

Mark Antony meets Cleopatra at Alexandria, Egypt, and they fall in love. He is called away by the death of his wife and the political situation in Rome. He resolves the conflict with Octavius Caesar by marrying Caesar's sister, Octavia, this makes Cleopatra deeply jealous.

Relations between Antony and Caesar soon deteriorate, and Antony returns to Egypt. Caesar follows with an army, and Antony is defeated. He hears a false report that Cleopatra is dead and falls on his sword; he dies in her arms. She is determined not to yield power to the conquering Caesar, so she takes her own life by the bite of a snake.

KEY QUOTATIONS

* Enobarbus on Cleopatra's first meeting with Mark Antony:

    The barge she sat in, like a burnish'd throne,
    Burn'd on the water; the poop was beaten gold,
    Purple the sails, and so perfumed, that
    The winds were love-sick with them, the oars were silver…

* Enobarbus on Cleopatra:

    Age cannot wither her, nor custom stale
    Her infinite variety

CORIOLANUS

This is a play about conflict and action. It has a harsh quality about it, with little lyrical poetry in the lines. It tells the story of many power struggles: between Rome and the neighbouring state of the Volsces, between Coriolanus and his enemy Aufidius and between the nobles of Rome and the common people. It is also the story of the struggle within Coriolanus – should he take revenge on the city that has rejected him, or should he take pity on his mother, his wife and his young son who are living there?

This is really a one-character play. The action centres entirely around Coriolanus. When he is not onstage at the centre of the action, he is the topic of discussion. He is a brave, heroic and supreme general, even compared with Hercules. What is more, he is honest and trustworthy – never manipulative, or jealous, and not hungry for power. But at the same time he is arrogant, over-dependent on his mother, and emotionally immature. He is yet another of Shakespeare's fascinatingly complex and human central characters.

The story
Coriolanus is so successful in battle that his fellow Romans decide to put him up for election as consul. Coriolanus speaks so contemptuously of the common people of Rome that he makes himself deeply unpopular,

and is banished. Furious, he goes straight to his arch enemy, Aufidius, and offers to lead his army against Rome. He does so, and at the walls of the city the Romans try to talk him out of his revenge attack. His mother, wife and son finally persuade him to leave Rome in peace. But Aufidius' people, the Volscians, accuse him of betraying them, and they kill him publicly.

JULIUS CAESAR

Here is one of Shakespeare's great plays. In subject matter, in characterization, and in language, it is rightly one of his most popular. He took as his source Plutarch's *Parallel Lives*, drawing on the accounts of the lives of Mark Antony, Marcus Brutus and Julius Caesar, and developed these three, along with Cassius, into complex characters.

The two key conspirators against Caesar, Cassius and Brutus, are entirely different people and differently motivated, but they are drawn together by a single purpose. Cassius is an envious man, who dislikes Caesar because of his success and his popularity. Brutus, on the other hand, is a republican who fears Caesar's power and believes that he must stop Caesar for the sake of the people of Rome.

Julius Caesar is also notable for its crowd scenes. In the democratic city of Rome, the opinion of the people was hugely important. However, the people are notoriously fickle and easily persuaded by rhetoric rather than by the deep political ideas which preoccupy the play's main characters. They are swayed back and forth by Brutus and Mark Antony, and won over finally by the better speaker: for all his protestations, Mark Antony is a more accomplished orator than Brutus.

The story

Worried that Caesar's ambition might lead him to strengthen his power over Rome too far, a group of conspirators led by Cassius and Brutus decide to assassinate Caesar. After the murder, Mark Antony, Caesar's friend, stirs the people up against Brutus. He, Octavius Caesar and Lepidus form a triumvirate (a coalition of three equal rulers). They make war on Cassius and Brutus, who are defeated at the battle of Philippi and kill themselves.

KEY CHARACTERS

Julius Caesar Popular dictator of Rome, who is assassinated half way through the play.

Marcus Brutus Caesar's friend, but he conspires against him for the greater good of Rome, as he sees it.

Caius Cassius The other leading conspirator, who first conceives the idea and persuades Brutus to join him.

Casca, Decius Brutus, Metellus Cimber and **Cinna** Some of the other members of the conspiracy.

Octavius Caesar, Mark Antony, and **Lepidus** Triumvirs after Caesar's death.

KEY QUOTATIONS

* Cassius on Caesar:
    Why, man, he doth bestride the narrow world
    Like a Colossus…

* Soothsayer:
    Beware the ides of March

* Calphurnia (Caesar's wife):
    When beggars die, there are no comets seen;
    The heavens themselves blaze forth the death of princes.

* Caesar:
    Cowards die many times before their deaths;
    The valiant never taste of death but once.

* Caesar's dying words:
    Et tu Brute? Then fall, Caesar!

* Mark Antony:
    Cry havoc and let slip the dogs of war

* Brutus justification for the murder:
    Not that I loved Caesar less, but that I loved Rome more

* Mark Anthony to the people of Rome:
    Friends, Romans, countrymen, lend me your ears;
    I come to bury Caesar, not to praise him…

* Mark Anthony describing the kill:
    This was the most unkindest cut of all.

PERICLES

This is arguably the worst of all Shakespeare's plays. However, he may
have an excuse for this. Shakespeare's company, the King's Men, did not
like to publish their plays because they wanted to retain their sole
rights. This is why several of the plays were pirated and printed as early
quartos. In the case of *Hamlet*, the King's Men responded by publish-
ing the official version. *Pericles*, however, was pirated in 1609 and the
company did not apparently produce an authorized version. *Pericles* is
also the only play missing from the First Folio of 1623 (perhaps the
original manuscript went missing). In any case, the only version we
have is the pirated one, which may have been very inaccurate.

The story

Pericles' life is in danger, so he flees the Phoenician seaport of Tyre. He
is shipwrecked at Pentapolis, where he wins the hand of the King's
daughter. When it is safe, they head back to Tyre but a storm brews, and
Pericles' wife goes into labour and gives birth to a daughter. His wife
appears dead, so he casts her into the sea in a wooden chest, but she is
rescued and ends up as a priestess of Diana. Pericles and his daughter
Marina survive, but she is later kidnapped. The whole family is now
separated. The remainder of the play tells the story of how they are
eventually reunited.

TIMON OF ATHENS

It is generally thought that this play was never finished, and that
Shakespeare meant to go back and revise it but never did. *Timon of
Athens* is a strange play, having no sub-plots and no real conflict, but
simply charting Timon's progress from people-lover to people-hater.
Timon starts the play with no close friends, and apparently no family,
and unlike almost every other of Shakespeare's leading characters, no
history – we don't know where his money came from, or anything
about his past. Even his death is a mystery. The play is more like a fable
or an allegorical tale.

The story

Timon is a noble and generous Athenian, who eventually spends all his wealth on his friends and is left with nothing. So he asks his richest friends to help him, but they refuse. Timon is deserted by all his friends and flatterers now that he has no money. He leaves Athens and goes to live alone in a cave where he muses on how he hates other people. He receives endless visitors whom he does not want. He becomes bitter and miserable, and eventually his tomb is found by the sea, bearing an inscription of hatred to all men.

TITUS ANDRONICUS

This is one of Shakespeare's earliest plays. It is quite likely that he was not solely responsible for it, although it is always attributed to him alone. In places it is more melodrama than anything else, with none of Shakespeare's later mastery of language.

The story

Tamora, Queen of the Goths, and her lover, Aaron the Moor, commit the most terrible crimes against the family of Titus Andronicus, a Roman general. Tamora's sons rape Titus' daughter and then cut out her tongue and cut off her hands so that she cannot name her attackers. After various other atrocities, Titus takes his revenge by killing Tamora's sons and serving them up to her in pie which she, unwittingly, eats.

TROILUS AND CRESSIDA

This is not actually a classical legend at all, although it is set in Troy; it is a medieval romance. Shakespeare's version of it, however, is as notable for its presentation of the reality and futility of war as for the love story at the centre of it. It is a difficult play to place in any category; it has at different times been regarded both as a comedy and as a tragedy.

Troilus is not in love so much with Cressida, as with the idea of being in love. He seduces her as soon as he can, and then expects her undying love in return. He does not seem to see what only Ulysses really sees – how fickle Cressida is by nature. Although she is only a young girl, Cressida is cunning from the start, knowing that the best way to win

Troilus is to play hard to get. She allows her scheming uncle, Pandarus, to talk her into sleeping with Troilus, but when Troilus is no longer around, she forgets him quickly in favour of Diomedes.

These games, almost playing at being in love, are echoed by the way the war is being conducted. It has its customs and its rules of chivalry, and when a truce is called, soldiers from both sides mix and enjoy an evening together. But is all fair in love and war? When Achilles finds Hector unarmed at the end of the day, thinking the battle is over until tomorrow, he breaks all convention and kills him.

KEY CHARACTERS

Priam King of Troy.

Troilus, Hector, Paris All sons of King Priam.

Cressida A young Trojan woman whose father is a traitor.

Pandarus Her uncle, a scheming go-between for Troilus and Cressida.

Agamemnon The Greek commander.

Ulysses, Achilles, Ajax Greek leaders and warriors.

The story

Pandarus acts as go-between between Priam's son Troilus and his own niece, Cressida, with whom Troilus has fallen in love. At Pandarus' persuasion, Cressida falls for Troilus and agrees (with little resistance) to sleep with him. They swear undying love to each other, but she later betrays him with Diomedes. He is disillusioned with women and leaves hurt and bitter. All this takes place against the backdrop of the Trojan War.

10 The Poems and Sonnets

THE SONNETS

Shakespeare's sonnets were not published until 1609, although many of them had been circulating for a while before then. One contemporary wrote in 1598 that Shakespeare was distributing 'sugared sonnets among his private friends'. But 1609 was their first public airing, when they were printed as a collection of 154 sonnets followed by a poem, *A Lover's Complaint*.

It is worth reading the sonnets in order, because there is a broad logical sequence to them, although they all stand alone. Some of them are written in pairs which both address the same subject; sometimes the second sonnet of the pair will even begin 'thus' or 'but', following on from the previous sonnet.

The sonnets are generally divided into three groups.

* Sonnets 1–126: These are all apparently addressed to a young man. They have an erotic edge to them, but they cover a wide range of topics, many of them neither sexual nor romantic. This group ends with a poem which is not technically a sonnet at all (having only twelve lines), which begins: 'O thou, my lovely boy…'.

* Sonnets 127–152: These seem to be written to a lady, generally known as the 'dark lady of the sonnets'. Scholars have made much of trying to identify who she might have been. The subject of these poems is the dark lady herself, Shakespeare's passion for her, and his feelings when she turns out to be unfaithful to him.

* Sonnets 153–154: The final pair of sonnets are quite unlike the first two groups, and are both imitations of Greek poems.

The collection of sonnets published in 1609 was dedicated to 'Mr WH'. This has led to extensive speculation about the identity of the young man in the first 126 sonnets, and the dark lady who is the subject of the next group of sonnets. But no answer has ever been conclusively found. There are plenty of candidates for 'WH', including Henry Wriothesley, Earl of Southampton, Shakespeare's patron, and various other people Shakespeare knew whose initials fit. Some even believe that the sonnets were written to Queen Elizabeth under another name.

In fact, it really doesn't matter who they were addressed to. Indeed, they may not have been autobiographical at all. The quality of the poems is such that their appeal is universal, regardless of who they were for. The best of the sonnets certainly rival the best poetry in any of Shakespeare's plays.

What is a sonnet?

A sonnet is a poem written to a very specific format. It must have fourteen lines, which are made up of three groups of four followed by a final pair. The three groups of four (known as quatraines) should each have two pairs of rhymes – in Shakespeare's case the first and third lines rhyme, as do the second and fourth. The final pair of lines (or couplet) should rhyme with each other.

So much for the shape of the poem – the content should also follow a set pattern.

* The first quatraine should establish the subject.

* The second quatraine should develop the theme.

* The third quatraine should round the theme off.

* The final pair of lines, or couplet, should sum up the whole sonnet.

For example, in Sonnet 94, the first quatraine describes the kind of person who has the power to do evil but chooses to be good; the second says how deserving these people are; the third goes on to say how evil acts from these people are worse than from anyone else; the final couplet rounds off the sonnet by summing up what has been said in the first twelve lines.

Sonnet 94

They that have power to hurt and will do none,
That do not do the thing they most do show,
Who, moving others, are themselves as stone,
Unmovèd, cold, and to temptation slow;
They rightly do inherit heaven's graces
And husband nature's riches from expense;
They are the lords and owners of their faces,
Others but stewards of their excellence.
The summer's flower is to the summer sweet,
Though to itself it only live and die;
But if that flower with base infection meet,
The basest weed outbraves his dignity:
For sweetest things turn sourest by their deeds;
Lilies that fester smell far worse than weeds.

The subject matter of the sonnets is extremely varied, from the obvious love poems to poems about the passage of time, nobility and having children. Some of the poems are quite bawdy and full of double meanings. Shakespeare often uses the word 'will', which as well as its surface meaning can also refer to himself by his diminutive Christian name. 'Will', however, clearly also has a phallic meaning, and this is obviously intended in some of the sonnets. Sonnet 135 is a good example of this: 'Whoever hath her wish, thou hast thy Will…'

Many of the sonnets are written in quite complex language, and are worth exploring. Even where the meaning is clear on the surface, the metaphors and imagery give the poem depth when you look at it more carefully. This sonnet, number 129, is obviously about lust, but worth a close reading to appreciate Shakespeare's writing fully. Even the punctuation is deliberate, giving a sense of the frenetic urgency of the pursuit of lust.

Sonnet 129

Th'expense of spirit in a waste of shame
Is lust in action, and, till action, lust
Is perjured, murd'rous, bloody, full of blame,
Savage, extreme, rude, cruel, not to trust,
Enjoyed no sooner but despised straight,
Past reason hunted, and no sooner had,
Past reason hated as a swallowed bait
On purpose laid to make the taker mad;
Mad in pursuit, and in possession so,
Had, having, and in quest to have, extreme,
A bliss in proof, and proved, a very woe,
Before, a joy proposed, behind, a dream.
All this the world well knows, yet none knows well
To shun the heaven that leads men to this hell.

The following sonnets are generally considered to be Shakespeare's finest; indeed among the finest poems ever written:

* Sonnet 18: Shall I compare thee to a summer's day…

* Sonnet 19: When, in disgrace with fortune and men's eyes…

* Sonnet 55: Not marble nor the gilded monuments…

* Sonnet 116: Let me not to the marriage of true minds…

* Sonnet 138: When my love swears that she is made of truth…

VENUS AND ADONIS

This poem was Shakespeare's most popular work during his own lifetime. He published it in 1593, and it appeared in nine different editions before his death. It was the work most often referred to by his contemporaries.

Venus and Adonis is a lewd, romantic poem written in stanzas, or (verses), of six lines each. It is written in a style that was very fashionable at the time, and drew on the Roman poet Ovid's classical work *Metamorphoses. Venus and Adonis* tells the story – in a somewhat flowery style – of the doomed mythical lovers of the title. Venus tries to persuade Adonis to meet her, but he cannot because he is hunting. She fails to dissuade him front the hunt and, next morning, hears his hounds. When she goes to look for Adonis, she finds him killed by the boar.

THE RAPE OF LUCRECE

This poem was published in 1594, a year after *Venus and Adonis*. Both of these were dedicated to the Earl of Southampton. This second poem, however, is over twice as long and more traditional, with a sombre and tragic theme. It tells of Lucrece, a virtuous wife, who is driven to suicide after being ravished by the lustful Tarquin.

Ironically, when Shakespeare wrote this poem, poetry was considered far more acceptable than drama when it came to literary reputation. Shakespeare no doubt thought at the time that if any work would make him famous beyond his own lifetime, it would be a poem such as this one.

A LOVER'S COMPLAINT

This is a complex poem, and not generally given the attention it deserves. It was first published in 1609, in the same volume as the collected sonnets. It tells the story of a young woman's seduction by an unscrupulous (but rather dashing) young man. The young woman herself relates the incident as she sits sobbing, tearing up papers, shrieking and generally behaving as if she is half mad. It has echoes of Ophelia in Hamlet, and of the song Desdemona sings at the end of *Othello*.

THE PHOENIX AND THE TURTLE

This poem was first published in 1601. It is a poem in two parts; thirteen four-line verses telling the story of the tragic love between the phoenix and the turtle dove (yes it's actually a dove, not a real turtle), followed by five three-line verses. It is an allegorical poem which tells how the phoenix and the turtle dove combined their two souls in one, and yet each remained individual.

THE PASSIONATE PILGRIM

This is actually an anthology of poems published in 1599 and attributed to Shakespeare on the title page. It includes some sonnets that are contained in the plays, some sonnets that were printed subsequently in the collected edition and some other poems that, although the whole book is attributed to Shakespeare, may not have been written by him. The best known of these is: 'Crabbèd age and youth cannot live together/ Youth is full of pleasance, age is full of care.'

It is a measure of Shakespeare's genius that even if he had not written a single play he would still rank as one of England's great poets.